HERITAGE
TRAILS IN
NORTH-WEST
ENGLAND

Cartmel Priory

HERITAGE TRAILS IN NORTH-WEST ENGLAND

BY

BRIAN CONDUIT

CICERONE PRESS

MILNTHORPE, CUMBRIA

© Brian Conduit
ISBN 1 85284 028 5
First Published 1989

CONTENTS

INTRODUCTION

The north-west of England is blessed with an extensive network of public footpaths which take walkers through a quite incredible variety of attractive, and at times spectacular, scenery. In addition the area possesses a similarly extensive variety of historic buildings and sites, from prehistoric monuments to Victorian mill villages, which reflect both its rich heritage and the role that it has played, throughout the centuries, in our national history.

Almost every day I am constantly aware of this dual attraction of fine scenery allied with historic interest. From my home in the Ribble Valley I look out from the back garden over a pleasant scene of fields and trees with the distinctive shape of Pendle Hill making a dramatic backcloth. In contrast, from my garden I can see the Norman keep of Clitheroe Castle framed by the Bowland Fells.

This book combines those twin features and describes a series of scenic walks that have an historic dimension and appeal, in order to add greater interest, variety, purpose and focal points to the pursuit of rambling in the countryside and in a few cases, towns. It arose out of a series of broadcasts that I have done for the B.B.C. Radio Lancashire in conjunction with their features producer, Judith Roberts, who asked me, back in 1984, to prepare a series of six programmes on the theme of local historic walks. At the outset I thought that we might be able to manage two such series, at the most, before running out of ideas and places to include. I could not have been more wrong. By discovering new possibilities and widening our geographical horizons to include the north-west as a whole (anywhere that can be reached on a day trip for most people within the Radio Lancashire area), we have already grown to five series with a further one prepared.

Although ranging over such a large and diverse region, the area covered by this book does have clearly defined boundaries - the lowland zones that encircle the predominantly hilly country of the north-west. In the north our limits are the Solway coastal plains dividing the north-west from Scotland, in the south the flat and fertile arable lands of Cheshire reaching down into the Midlands and to the borders of Wales, and in the east the Vale of York, more of a natural dividing line between north-west and north-east England than the more commonly used Pennines, although this might well be disputed by Yorkshire folk. In the west the boundary is of course both undisputed and obvious - the Irish Sea coast.

Within the confines of this fairly substantial slice of the country, the walks encompass an enormously wide range of scenery and terrain. We ramble through the mountains and lakes of Cumbria, the moorlands and wooded valleys of the Yorkshire Dales, the bare uplands of the South Pennines and forests of Rossendale and Bowland, the lush greenery of the Ribble and Hodder valleys and Cheshire parklands, and sections of the west coast stretching from the shores of Morecambe Bay and the Kent estuary in the north, down via the Lune estuary and the Fylde, to the Wirral and Dee estuary in the south.

If anything the historic sites visited during the course of these walks are even more varied. They embrace prehistoric stone circles, Roman forts, medieval castles and manor houses, monastic remains, great country houses, industrial monuments and museums, two of the great historic cities of the north-west and places associated with the lives of some of the greatest figures in our literary heritage.

All the walks are on public rights of way or permitted paths and are of modest length and difficulty, well within the capabilities of anyone of average fitness. No special clothing or equipment is required, apart from strong footwear - ideally walking boots - and waterproofs to combat the fickle north-west weather. On most of the walks the greatest hazard likely to be encountered, especially during the winter months, is mud.

By following some of these 'heritage trails', you will not only see some marvellous scenery and have a lot of enjoyment but you should also acquire a new perspective on the historic development of north-west England. By the end of most of these walks, you will find that the north-west is not only blessed with scenic and historic attractions but also with an abundance of pubs and cafés, tea rooms and coffee shops - a most welcome bonus.

GENERAL INFORMATION

1. The approximate time given at the start of each walk is based on walking at a moderate pace and not stopping too often, apart from exploring the historic sites. If you intend to have frequent stops, indulge in lengthy refreshment breaks and spend a long time at each site (all highly-recommended pastimes) then allow for a much longer period.

2. Some of the sites visited in the course of these walks can be viewed

freely all the year round. Most have an admission charge and limited opening hours and a few have very restricted opening times. Details of these and telephone numbers for information on those that have restricted opening times and/or admission charges are given below.

No admission charge and open all the time
Castlerigg Stone Circle (Walk 1), Hardknott Fort (Walk 3), Jervaulx Abbey (Walk 5 - honesty box), Bolton Priory and Barden Tower (Walk 6), Piel Castle (Walk 7), Clitheroe Castle (Walk 8), Cartmel Priory (Walk 9), Arnside Tower (Walk 12), Chester - Cathedral, St. John's Church and Roman Amphitheatre (Walk 13), Lancaster Priory (Walk 15), Heysham - Church and St. Patrick's Chapel (Walk 16), Cockersand Abbey (Walk 17).

Restricted opening and/or admission charges
A. ENGLISH HERITAGE PROPERTIES
Admission charges vary according to the size and popularity of the building but opening times are fairly standard.

| 15 March - 14 October 9.30-6.30 weekdays | 2.00-6.30 Sundays |
| 15 October - 14 March 9.30-4.00 weekdays | 2.00-4.00 Sundays |

If you wish to be absolutely sure, a phone call either to the building itself or to the local Tourist Information Centre will give you full details.

English Heritage properties included in the book: Richmond Castle and Easby Abbey (Walk 4), Middleham Castle (Walk 5), Furness Abbey (Walk 7) and Chester Castle (Walk 13).

B. STATELY HOMES
Most of these are closed during the winter months and some may have very restricted opening times during the summer period.

Holker Hall (Walk 2)	044853 328
Tatton Park (Walk 18)	0565 54822
Turton Tower (Walk 19)	0204 852203
Hoghton Tower (Walk 20)	025485 2986
Rufford Old Hall (Walk 21)	0704 821254
Lyme Park (Walk 22)	0663 62023
Harewood House (Walk 23)	0532 886225
Browsholme Hall (Walk 26)	025486 330

C. REMAINDER
(CASTLES, ABBEYS, MUSEUMS, VISITOR CENTRES)

Ribchester Museum (Walk 2)	025484 261
Whalley Abbey (Walk 8)	025482 2268
Fountains Abbey (Walk 10)	076586 333
Bolton Castle (Walk 11)	0969 23981/23674
Thurstaston Visitor Centre (Walk 14)	051 648 4371
Lancaster Castle (Walk 15)	0524 64998
Lancaster Maritime Museum (Walk 15)	0524 64637
Dove Cottage, Grasmere (Walk 28)	09665 544
Rydal Mount, Rydal (Walk 28)	05394 3002
Bronte Parsonage, Haworth (Walk 29)	0535 42323
Quarry Bank Mill, Styal (Walk 32)	0625 527468
Helmshore Textile Museums (Walk 33)	0706 226459
Wigan Pier (Walk 36)	0942 44888

Two useful annual publications that give full details of current admission charges and opening times are:

Historic Houses, Castles and Gardens in Great Britain and Ireland (British Leisure Publications)

2,000 Places to Visit in Britain (A.A. Publications)

3. All the walks are easy to follow but remember that the countryside is an ever changing phenomenon: hedges are sometimes dug up, stiles fall into disrepair, new fences appear and footpaths can become slightly re-routed. Therefore it is possible that by the time you do these walks, some minor changes to the route directions may have occurred. If this is so, they are likely to be clearly indicated and cause you no problems.

4. Please observe the Country Code whenever and wherever you are out walking, for the sake of those for whom the countryside is their source of livelihood, as well as your source of pleasure and recreation.

Guard against all risk of fire;

Fasten all gates;

Keep dogs under proper control;

Keep to the paths across farm land;

Avoid damaging fences, hedges and walls

Leave no litter;
Safeguard water supplies;
Protect wildlife, wild plants and trees;
Go carefully on country roads;
Respect the life of the countryside.

PREHISTORIC AND ROMAN HERITAGE

Physical factors e.g. climate, terrain, geographical location, have played a major role in the moulding of the history of the north-west. The most densely populated areas of prehistoric Britain were the chalk uplands of Hampshire, Dorset and Wiltshire, because our early ancestors found their comparatively dry and warm slopes preferable for settlement, farming and communications to either the surrounding thickly-wooded lowlands, or the wetter and colder moorland and mountains further north and west. Therefore the major prehistoric monuments are in the south, but nevertheless there are a number of substantial remains in the north-west, especially in Cumbria.

The Romans likewise built most of their civilian settlements and villas in the drier, warmer and more fertile lowland areas of the south and east. To them the north was a frontier area, a military zone, where they built a series of forts, of which the most important were the great legionary fortresses of Deva (Chester) and Eboracum (York). These forts were built both to contain the native tribes of the north and to protect Roman Britain from raiders outside the imperial frontiers in Scotland and Ireland. Straight, well-constructed roads linked the forts with each other and with the ultimate defence of Hadrian's Wall.

The first group of walks include the most impressive prehistoric site in north-west England and two Roman forts - one of which occupies a particularly wild and dramatic location at the head of Eskdale and near the far north-western frontier of the empire.

1. CASTLERIGG STONE CIRCLE

Start and Finish: Keswick
Distance: 7 miles   *Approximate Time:* 3hrs 30 mins
Ordnance Survey Landranger Map: 90
Parking: Lakeside car park, just outside (and signposted from) Keswick town centre.
Refreshments: Plenty of pubs, restaurants and cafes in Keswick.

General Description
Keswick lies amidst some of the most majestic mountain terrain in England and the finest features of Lakeland scenery are all combined in this walk: woodland, lake and fell. All the way there are glorious views over the surrounding lakes and mountains and a prehistoric stone circle forms the main historic interest. Two modest climbs are encountered - a lengthy one up the thickly wooded slopes of Walla Crag and a short one to the summit of Castle Head, from where there is a magnificent view across Derwentwater.

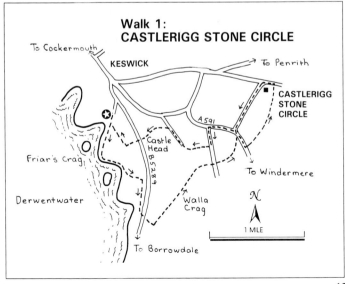

Walk 1:
CASTLERIGG STONE CIRCLE

Route Directions (Keswick to Castlerigg Stone Circle)
As one of the main tourist centres of the Lake District, it is difficult to think of Keswick as an industrial town, but in the 16th century it was the hub of an important mining district. Elizabeth I even imported skilled German miners to work the local mines (chiefly iron and lead) but in the 17th century most of the mining finished and closed down. There was a revival in the 18th century with the mining of graphite or plumbago, the basis of Keswick's best known industry, pencil manufacturing, but this also was worked out in the 19th century. The last graphite was mined in 1838 but the pencil and crayon industry survived.

In the town centre the major building is the Moot Hall, built in 1813 on the site of an earlier Elizabethan building. The upper floor was the council chamber and the ground floor a market - now the building serves Keswick's most flourishing modern industry, as a Tourist Information Centre.

The first part of the walk is along the road from the car park to the lake, past the landing stage for the motor launches and on along the woodland track that leads to the end of Friar's Crag, one of the Lake District's most popular and frequently photographed beauty spots. The reason for its popularity is evident - the views across the lake to Catbells and the array of peaks above the western side of Derwentwater and down the whole length of the lake into Borrowdale.

From the end of the promontory, you follow a path round to the left, through a gate and along the lakeside path, over two footbridges

*Castlerigg
Stone Circle
about the turn
of the century
(Abbot Hall Art
Gallery, Kendal)*

and turning left through a gate into a wood. Keep along the path by the edge of the wood, over another footbridge, bear right, go through a gate at the end of the wood and turn left along the broad path up to the Borrowdale road. Turn right along the path through the trees that runs parallel to the road and, after about 0.5 mile, the path joins the road at Calfclose Bay (National Trust sign).

Turn right along the road for a few yards, cross over and go through a gap in the opposite wall, bearing right along a path that leads up through the trees to a car park. Go straight across the car park to a stile and gate, climb over, or go through and continue uphill, turning right at a T-junction of paths. Almost immediately you turn sharp left, following the National Trust sign to Walla Crag, and taking the uphill path through thick conifer woods. The path is fairly steep but straight, well surfaced and easy to follow. Gaps in the trees on the left give fine views over Keswick, Bassenthwaite and on the horizon, Skiddaw. After 0.5 mile the path levels out and descends to a junction of paths. Here you take the right-hand one (signposted Rakefoot and Walla Crag) and climb again for a short while, bearing right to a stile.

After climbing it you leave the woods and, for the time being, any more climbing. Being in open country now you get extensive and uninterrupted views in all directions for much of the rest of the way. Keep ahead along a path between a wall on the right and a wire fence on the left and, when you come to a mini ravine, turn right, through a gate and along the right-hand edge of the ravine. Go through another gate and keep on ahead, following the path down to a footbridge where

15

gate and keep on ahead, following the path down to a footbridge where you turn left over the bridge and head up steps to a gate. Go through, turn left and join the lane in front of you.

Keep to the left along a lane for a few yards, and then turn right at a ladder stile and gate (public footpath sign to Dale Bottom and Castlerigg Stone Circle) along a grassy sunken path. In front are superb panoramic mountain views, taking in the peaks of High Dod, High Rigg, Blencathra and Skiddaw. Continue over a stile and along the edge of a field (wall on left), ahead and over (or through) the next stile (or gate) and turn left (wall on left) along the edge of the next field to a ladder stile and gate. Keep along the edge of the next field to another ladder stile and gate, and through the next field to a gate which brings you to the main Keswick-Windermere road (A591).

Turn right along the road for a few yards and then first left along a track, past some houses, and keep in a straight line over a succession of stiles eventually reaching a lane by a wood. Turn left and Castlerigg Stone Circle is in the field on the left.

Castlerigg Stone Circle
This is one, and probably the most visually impressive of a number of prehistoric circles scattered throughout Cumbria and the north-west, but the problem is that little is known about any of them. Castlerigg was first excavated in 1882 and comprises 38 stones grouped in an oval rather than true circle, about 100 to 110 feet in diameter, with a further 10 stones outside the circle to the south-east which form a rectangle.

No one really knows when it was built. It could be Neolithic or Bronze Age, possibly erected around 1500 B.C. or even earlier. Despite being sometimes referred to as the Druids Circle, it is definitely older than the druids. Again we are not sure what it was for but, like the larger and better known circles at Stonehenge and other sites in the south, it probably had a religious significance.

The setting is magnificent and the stones certainly exert a powerful and mysterious atmosphere, theatrically situated on a plateau and ringed by mountains which form a natural amphitheatre. All we can do is stand and gaze in admiration at the skills of our supposedly primitive ancestors, before returning to Keswick.

Route Directions (Castlerigg Stone Circle to Keswick)
Along the edge of the field in which the stones are situated is a narrow

along the lane for 0.5 mile back to the A591. Turn right along the road (there is a footpath at the side of it) and follow it for 0.5 mile. A few yards after the Keswick sign, turn left along a lane (signposted to Castlerigg and Rakefoot) and, just past a house on the right, turn right through a gate (public footpath sign) and along a narrow path between a wall on the left and a wire fence on the right. Follow the path to the left and right (fine view of Walla Crag to the left and across Derwent Water in front), under a bridge and downhill through woodland.

Cross the footbridge over Brockle Beck, turn right and follow the path by the stream downhill, through a gate and ahead past a farm and over a bridge. The farm track now becomes a tarmac lane which you keep along, passing houses on the right for nearly 0.5 mile. When you see a footpath sign to Castle Head, turn left along the narrow path (between a hedge on the right and fence on the left) and go through a gate at the end, continue up the steps ahead into woodland. Keep on, climbing gently all the time (there are several paths) through the woods, to emerge eventually at the top. Pause here to take a rest and enjoy one of the Lake District's finest views - a magnificent vista of lakes and mountains looking across Derwent Water, Keswick and Bassenthwaite.

When you can tear yourself away, descend back into the trees, following the lower slopes of the hill round to the left to pick up a path that continues to bear left down to a gate and steps, on to the Borrowdale road. Cross over to a gap in the wall opposite, go down more steps and walk along the straight path ahead. When it enters woodland, turn right along the edge of the wood and the path takes you back to the car park.

Stonyhurst College

2. RIBCHESTER FORT, STYDD CHAPEL AND STONYHURST COLLEGE

Start and Finish: Ribchester
Distance: 8 miles   *Approximate Time:* 4 hours
Ordnance Survey Landranger Map: 103
Parking: Ribchester
Refreshments: Pubs and cafes in Ribchester and Hurst Green, Miles House Farm Restaurant by Ribchester Bridge.

General Description
A splendid walk amidst the glorious scenery of the Ribble Valley. It takes you from Lancashire's major Roman remains, past a small and almost unknown ex-monastic church, to a great 17th century house that was involved both in the English Civil War and the French Revolution, and is now one of the principal Roman Catholic schools in the country.

Ribchester Fort

The Roman fort is near the car park and is clearly signposted. Although there is little to see above ground level, the fort at Ribchester (Latin name *Bremetennacum*) is the principal Roman monument in Lancashire. It was built around 78 A.D. at the time that the Roman conquerors were slowly pushing the frontiers of their power northwards and westwards into the more remote and wild regions of the new province.

It was a cavalry fort covering approximately 6 acres most of which remains unexcavated. Some of it will never see the light of day because, since Roman times, the Ribble has changed its course and the present river bed occupies the south-east corner of the fort. The medieval church and its churchyard also cover much of the fort. Ribchester was an important post on the north-south route between Manchester and Hadrian's Wall and on the east-west route across to the forts at Ilkely and York. In its early days the fort was defended by a ditch and earth rampart, later rebuilt in stone. It was of the usual playing-card shape that was common to almost all Roman forts throughout the empire.

The granary or storehouse with its hypocaust (underfloor heating system) is the only part that is visible. Many of the objects discovered in excavations are on display in the museum on the site, but the

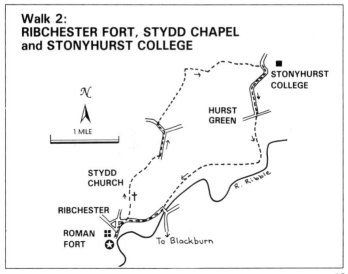

Walk 2:
RIBCHESTER FORT, STYDD CHAPEL
and STONYHURST COLLEGE

principal find, a superb Roman helmet, is in the British Museum in London, although there is a replica at Ribchester.

Route Directions (Ribchester Fort to Stydd Chapel)
Walk up the main street, past the 'White Bull' whose portico columns were fished out of the Ribble and are thought to have come from the Roman fort, and turn right along the road signposted to Blackburn. Just past the 'New Hotel' and opposite the Stonebridge Restaurant, turn left along a broad track which you follow past the early 18th century Stydd almshouses, built by the Shireburns of Stonyhurst to house five poor people, and up to Stydd Chapel.

Stydd Chapel
This tiny church, standing on its own amidst farms and grazing land, is all that remains of a monastery belonging to the Knights Hospitallers of St. John of Jerusalem. The Knights Hospitallers were a crusading and military order founded in 1113 with the object of providing assistance and protection to pilgrims visiting the Holy Land. They had about 56 small monasteries, called commanderies, scattered throughout England, but by the time of Henry VIII's dissolution of the monasteries in the 1530's, only 15 remained.

Stydd was dissolved around 1338. The chapel still retains some 12th century Norman work and contains effigies of some of the knights.

Route Directions (Stydd Chapel to Stonyhurst College)
Continue along the track past the chapel, go through a farmyard, over a stile and then bear right across the field keeping close to the wire fence and hedge on the right. Near the wood climb two stiles and continue, with hedge and trees on the right, to a stile which admits you to Duddel Wood. Follow the path through the trees down to the footbridge over Duddel Brook, cross over and turn left. Follow the brook through a particularly attractive stretch of woodland before turning right opposite the next footbridge and climbing steeply up to the top of the ridge. Climb the stile at the top and head across the field towards the farm ahead of you, where you climb a stile and turn left along the road.

At this point there are fine views across the Ribble Valley to Pendle Hill on the right. Walk along the road to the first junction, turn left, and, near the first houses on the left, turn right along a wide farm track. Go through a gate, past the farm, through another gate and carry on by a wire fence to the left. Cross a footbridge and bear left to follow the edge of the next field, keeping close to the wire fence on the left. Turn left over a stile in that fence and head straight across the field towards a farm in front and a marvellous view of Pendle. Climb a stile in a wire fence and walk on, climb another stile (not easy to see but where there is a gap between bushes and a barbed wire fence) and continue towards the left-hand side of the farm where you turn left through a gate to follow an uphill path through a wood. At the top, where you come out of the wood, go through a gate and, bearing slightly to the left, make your way downhill toward a farm. In front is a splendid view over Longridge Fell.

Before reaching the farm turn right sharply at a stone wall and follow the clear track ahead, climbing a stile and keeping by the boundary wall of a wood on the left. Climb another stile, go past a farm and shortly afterwards look out for a stile on the left between the end of a wire fence and start of a wall. Climb it, immediately climb a ladder-stile in front, turn left keeping to the edge of the wood, climb another ladder-stile and follow the path very steeply down to a footbridge over a stream. Cross over and climb up the equally steep bank opposite to a stile, climb over and carry on straight ahead to a farm. Go through the farmyard and, in front of the house, turn right and head downhill towards the corner of the woods in front. Climb a stile, cross a footbridge and climb another stile which admits you to what was the Deer Park of the Stonyhurst Estate. Carry on by a wire fence on the right and then head straight across the open parkland, taking care to dodge balls as this is now a golf course, to the far left-hand corner. Go through the gate on to the road and Stonyhurst College is in front.

Stonyhurst College
The home of the Shireburn family since the 14th century, most of the buildings at Stonyhurst belong to the great house that was started by Sir Richard Shireburn in 1592. He was an enterprising and ambitious man who played an active role in the service of the Tudor monarchs as Chief Forester of Bowland, Lieutenant of the Isle of Man, Deputy Lieutenant of Lancashire and one of Henry VIII's commissioners of enquiry into the state of the monasteries, eagerly participating in the suppression of Whalley Abbey. Despite this he embraced the new Protestant religion of Elizabeth I rather half-heartedly and his succes-

sors, like so many aristocratic Lancashire families, reverted to the traditional Catholic faith and on several occasions Stonyhurst and its owners were suspected of being involved in Catholic plots. During the Civil War, Oliver Cromwell stayed here both before and after the Battle of Preston in August 1648 where he routed Royalist armies from Scotland and north-west England. Such an ardent Parliamentarian and Puritan was not exactly a welcome guest in the home of a staunch Royalist and Catholic family, and it is said that on both occasions Cromwell slept on the table with pistols at his side and men on guard around him.

Sir Richard's house was completed in the early 17th century and most of the south front belongs to this period. The gardens were laid out towards the end of the 17th century when some extensions to the house were also made. In the 18th century the house passed by marriage first to the Norfolk family and then to the Welds of Lulworth, who neglected Stonyhurst in favour of their main Dorset residence.

After the Protestant Reformation an English Catholic college, run by the Jesuits, had been set up on the continent, first in France and later in Flanders. During the anti-religious fervour of the French Revolution, the Jesuits were expelled and in 1794 Thomas Weld offered them the half-ruined Stonyhurst as a refuge. They accepted gladly, restored the original building and considerably extended it during the 19th century, adding the church (built in the style of King's College Chapel at Cambridge) in the 1830's. The result is that today Stonyhurst College ranks as one of the foremost Roman Catholic boarding schools in the country, a fitting role for a house that once belonged to one of the principal Catholic families in the north-west.

Route Directions (Stonyhurst College to Ribchester Fort)
Follow the road through the college grounds down into Hurst Green and, on the right-hand side of the 'Shireburn Arms', take the track signposted to Dinckley Ferry. The rest of the route is relatively easy to follow as it is waymarked with Ribble Way signs. With fine views of the Ribble Valley in front, follow the track down to the river, through a farmyard, through a gate and continue parallel to the river. Do **not** go over the stile on the left down to Dinckley Ferry but carry straight on over a stile, along the edge of a field to a gate and stile, over that and on to a stream. Cross over and bear right along the edge of the next field, following it as it curves uphill and to the left to a stile in the far

corner.

Climb over, go straight across the farm track to another stile, over that and, keeping in a roughly straight line, go over two more stiles, bearing right after the second one along the edge of a field, following it round to the trees ahead. Turn right over a stile and head downhill, bearing right over another stile and down through the trees to the riverbank where you turn right. Keep by the Ribble, at first through woodland and later across meadows, as far as a ladder-stile on the right. Climb over, continue straight on for a few yards and then turn left in front of a farmhouse to join a broad track.

Follow this track up to Ribchester Bridge and continue along the road back to Ribchester village.

Hardknott Fort amidst the fells of upper Eskdale

3. HARDKNOTT FORT

Start and Finish: Birks Bridge - 2 miles north of Seathwaite in the Duddon Valley.

Distance: 7 miles   *Approximate Time:* 4 hours

Ordnance Survey Landranger Maps: 90 and 96

Parking: Forestry Commission Car Park near Birks Bridge.

Refreshments: None

General Description

A magnificent scenic walk around the slopes of Harter Fell (2,140 feet) amidst the rugged grandeur of one of the wildest and least known areas of the Lake District. The outward route climbs out of the Duddon Valley and drops down to the remains of a Roman fort perched high up overlooking Eskdale, while the return journey leads over bare fellsides before descending through forest back to the Duddon. Inevitably some rough uphill work is involved: one short climb and a second lengthier one, but neither of them too steep or strenuous.

Route Directions (Birks Bridge to Hardknott Fort)

From the car park cross the bridge over the River Duddon and turn right along the grassy riverside path. Where the trees end on the left, climb a stile and carry on keeping close to the river, before bearing left towards a farm. Just before the farm buildings, turn sharp left through a gate, cross the field towards a group of rocks and, by the rocks, go through a gate in the wall and turn left. Continue by the side of the wall for about 100 yards and then bear right uphill towards the edge of conifer plantations.

As you proceed upwards take time to stop and turn for superb views over the Duddon Valley. The path is not very clear but head towards the trees, keeping to the right of the wall bordering the plantation. Cross the ladder-stile in a wall ahead and continue to the top of the ridge, veering slightly to the right after reaching the end of the trees. At the top you get a magnificent view down the whole length of Eskdale with the Roman fort visible below, its distinctive playing-card shape standing out clearly. Drop down to the road (this is the notorious Hardknott Pass), turn left and, where the road takes a sharp hairpin bend to the left, keep on along a faint path towards the fort. It is best to keep to the higher ground to the right where you cross the parade ground (a flattish area free from boulders), before entering the fort by the east gateway.

Hardknott Fort
The approximately 500 auxiliary troops who manned the Roman fort of Mediobogdum came mainly from Dalmatia, in present day Yugoslavia. It is not difficult to image what they thought about serving in

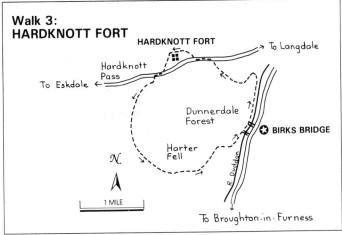

Walk 3:
HARDKNOTT FORT

this remote, rainy, windswept spot high up on the north-western outpost of the Roman Empire, far removed from the warm climate of their native shores. Bleak it may be, and certainly inhospitable as a place to live, but the scenery is majestic and awe-inspiring and the building of the fort in this difficult location is a triumph of Roman engineering.

Hardknott Fort was built around the end of the 1st, and beginning of the 2nd century, to guard the route over the mountains linking the forts of Ravenglass and Ambleside, via Eskdale and Langdale. Like all Roman forts, whether in Britain, Spain or Egypt, it was built on the conventional playing-card design, with gateways along each of the four walls and the usual internal arrangement of Principia (headquarters building) Praetorium (commander's house), granaries and barracks. The walls were originally 12 feet high, with battlements and taller corner towers. Even in such a comparatively small and inaccessible fort as this, the Roman troops enjoyed the luxury of a bath house, the remains of which lie just outside the walls to the south.

Route Directions (Hardknott Fort to Birks Bridge)

At the lower end of the fort follow the path down to the road and turn right. By the first group of trees and just before a cattle-grid, turn left over a footbridge (public footpath sign to Eskdale and Muncaster), turn right to climb two stiles in quick succession and then follow the clear and fairly straight path ahead which climbs steadily, giving superlative views over Eskdale to the right and Harter Fell to the left.

Near a stream go through a gate in a wall, keep on to re-cross the wall shortly by another gate and continue along the path. At this point it becomes more difficult to follow but, if you keep roughly parallel with the fence on the right, you cannot go wrong. Eventually after 1.5 miles of steady uphill walking, the route flattens out and reaches the edge of the Forestry Commission plantation of Dunnerdale Forest. Enter the forest via a gate and follow a blue waymarked track downhill through the trees. Near the end of a forest road bear left where the paths fork and continue, later to rejoin the forest road. Where the road bends sharply to the right keep on (blue waymark) and, at a junction of paths, turn right downhill to the forest road again.

Leaving the forest, cross over the road and take the track ahead leading to a farm. Go through the gate, keeping to the left of the farm buildings, and bear left through another gate to follow a path through a small wood down towards the river. Near the river you can make a short diversion to the right to see Birks Bridge, a picturesque pack-horse bridge over the rocky, gushing waters of the Duddon. On the south side of the bridge the clear, deep pools are a decidedly green colour. Return to the car park by following the grassy path on the left.

MEDIEVAL HERITAGE

The frontier theme continues into the Middle Ages and the northwest has a particularly rich legacy from this period. To medieval English kings the north-west was one of the most vital strategic areas of their kingdom, facing the three potentially hostile Celtic areas of Scotland to the north, Wales to the south-west and Ireland across the sea.

Not surprisingly the area is dotted with castles, from the early simple stone keeps erected by the Norman conquerors in the late 11th and early 12th centuries to the more complex structures of the later Middle Ages. On a smaller scale are the numerous pele towers, unique to this area and the neighbouring north-east. These were basically 'mini castles' - small fortified towers built as protection from Scottish raids, chiefly in the 14th and 15th centuries when such raids were especially frequent. Many of the later great houses of the region grew out of these originally simple, dark and cramped structures.

The other great monuments of the medieval period are ecclesiastical: the abbeys and priories, some of the finest of which are in the Yorkshire Dales. Despite its lawlessness and vulnerability to Scottish raids the north-west was favoured by certain monastic orders, notably the Cistercians and Premonstratensians whose foundations are particularly widespread throughout the area, because it possessed the remoteness and seclusion they desired. The north-west also possessed rich sheep pastures and mineral deposits - sources of much of the wealth amassed by the larger monasteries and a major reason for their ultimate decline and fall.

The following walks embrace many of the well-known castles, monasteries and manor houses of the Middle Ages. Most are in ruins: the castles and smaller fortified buildings because the advent of gunpowder rendered them largely obsolete (and also because their owners were looking for greater comfort once the country became more settled), and the monasteries because Henry VIII's wholesale closures in the 1530s ended them, apart from the odd case where the abbey church was preserved as the local parish church.

Richmond Castle high above the River Swale

4. RICHMOND CASTLE AND EASBY ABBEY

Start and Finish: Richmond
Distance: 3.5 miles   *Approximate Time:* 1hr 30mins
Ordnance Survey Landranger Maps: 92 and 99
Parking: Richmond
Refreshments: Pubs, restaurants and cafes in Richmond

General Description

Like many of the Yorkshire Dales, Swaledale has a ruined castle and abbey situated close to each other and linked by riverside paths. This easy stroll through woods and across meadows includes fine views of both the ruins and the surrounding valley. As it is short, the walk leaves plenty of time at the end to explore the narrow streets and alleys of Richmond, one of the most interesting and picturesque towns in the country.

Route Directions (Richmond Castle to Easby Abbey)

From the top end of Richmond's spacious Market Place walk down past All Saint's Church to the bottom end, and turn right along Millgate. Bear left and right downhill to the river and, at a small car park, turn left by the weir to join the riverside path. Keeping close to the river, walk across a picnic area, under a bridge and straight on, following the path round to the left where it turns sharply away from the river. After 50 yards turn right along a broad track through the woods that clothe the steep cliffs above the Swale.

The woods are most attractive and the path gives fine views upstream of Richmond town and castle, soon dropping down to rejoin the riverbank for just under 0.5 mile. On approaching Easby go up some steps, climb a stile and make your way to the abbey ruins clearly visible in front.

Easby Abbey

Easby Abbey was founded in 1155 as a house of Premonstratensian canons. Canons were technically priests not monks, but as they lived a monastic type of existence the difference between them was very slight. Like the Cistercians, the Premonstratensians sought solitude and they certainly found it in this idyllic spot on the banks of the Swale. As a result of its isolation, Easby had a fairly uneventful history up to its dissolution in 1536 though, like most northern monasteries, it suffered from raids by both Scottish and English armies during the frequent Scottish wars of the later Middle Ages.

The sloping, narrow site between hill and river on which it is built necessitated an unusual plan which can initially be confusing. Most of

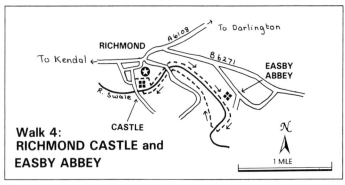

Walk 4:
RICHMOND CASTLE and EASBY ABBEY

the domestic buildings are grouped around the cloisters on the south side of the church as usual, but the large infirmary block lies to the north of the church. The church is the least substantial surviving portion - not much is left apart from the presbytery - but there are extensive remains of the infirmary, refectory and dormitory.

Next to the ruins stands the small 13th century parish church and beyond that the abbey gatehouse. Since the canons of Easby were not monks, they could take part in parochial duties and, until the dissolution, served as the local priests.

Route Directions (Easby Abbey to Richmond Castle)
On leaving the ruins first make a short detour up the lane in order to enjoy the superb view of the abbey, lying below amidst riverside meadows, and Richmond Castle in the distance dominating the whole area.

Return downhill and turn left to continue along the riverside path through another stretch of attractive woodland. Where the path forks, bear slightly left along the higher one and turn right to cross a disused railway bridge over the river. The route now follows the track of the former railway back to Richmond. Gaps in the hedges that line both sides reveal more views of Easby Abbey and the approach to the town is particularly impressive.

Just before coming out on to the road near a bridge, turn right down some steps to the riverbank, turn left under the bridge and over a stile to follow a path by the river. Bearing slightly left uphill away from the river, climb a stile, keep straight on and, near some trees, climb another stile. The path continues downhill through the trees back to the river from which there are superb views of the castle, towering above its rocky cliff on the opposite bank. At the next bridge turn right over the river and continue, turning right up steep Cornforth Hill, through a gate in one of the few remaining sections of Richmond's medieval walls, and along The Bar to the Market Place and on to the castle entrance.

Richmond Castle
Despite its powerful and forbidding appearance, Richmond Castle has had a history scarcely any less tranquil than that of Easby Abbey. It was away from the main lines of communication, never besieged and involved neither in the Wars of the Roses nor in the Civil Wars of the 17th century. Its present ruined state is more the result of decay and

neglect than deliberate destruction.

It was founded in the late 11th century soon after the Norman Conquest by Alan the Red of Brittany, one of William the Conqueror's followers. Until the 14th century it remained in the possession of the dukes of Brittany, which caused problems because of the many wars between England and France, and it was forfeited to the Crown on several occasions. It was later held by various royal dukes and in 1485 came fully under Crown ownership when Henry Tudor, Earl of Richmond, became King Henry VII.

The castle occupies a large triangular area on a cliff above the river and commands the entrance to Swaledale. Its curtain walls are virtually intact and the late 12th century keep, over 100 feet high, is one of the best preserved and tallest in the country. Particularly noteworthy is the two-storied Scolland's Hall, part of Alan the Red's original 11th century castle and one of the earliest surviving domestic buildings.

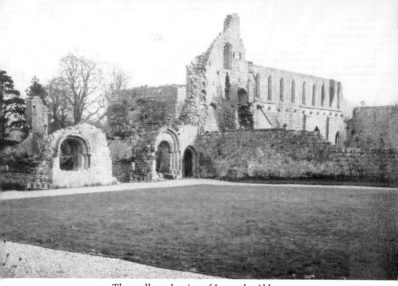

The mellowed ruins of Jervaulx Abbey

5. JERVAULX ABBEY AND MIDDLEHAM CASTLE

Start and Finish: Jervaulx Abbey - on the A6108 about 5 miles north of Masham.
Distance: 9 miles   *Approximate Time:* 5 hours
Ordnance Survey Landranger Map: 99
Parking: Jervaulx Abbey
Refreshments: Pubs and cafes in Middleham, Cover Bridge Inn.

General Description
This walk through Wensleydale, widest and gentlest of the Yorkshire Dales, links a picturesque ruined abbey and a forbidding-looking castle, stronghold of Richard III, by field and riverside paths. All the way the views across the dale are superb and the return route is mostly along the wooded banks of the Cover and Ure, making a particularly pleasant and relaxing finale.

Route Directions (Jervaulx Abbey to Middleham Castle)
Turn right out of the car park along the main road and after 0.25 mile take the first lane on the right (signposted to Ellingstring and Healey). Follow it round to the left and uphill for 0.75 mile and, where the lane

levels off, turn right along the track to Hammer Farm. This broad track follows the lower slopes of Witton Fell on the left and gives sweeping views across Wensleydale to the right.

Go through the farmyard keeping to the left of the house and, just past the house, bear right through a gate and across the field. There is no clear path but head in the direction of the tower of East Witton church in front. Go through a gate by a wall and keep straight on to pick up a distinct path again which you follow downhill, through another gate and right by the side of a stream in a small ravine to the left. Go through the gate in front, over the stream and continue along a clear track (that later becomes surfaced) which descends past farms and cottages into the village of East Witton. In the village turn left along the side of the very long and wide green (about 0.25 mile long), lined on both sides by attractive stone cottages.

At the end of the green keep going along the lane for a few yards, turn right through the first gate and immediately left across the field, making for a barn ahead. Although the paths on the next section of the walk are not very clear in parts, the route is conveniently waymarked with arrows. Go through a gate by the barn and across the next field, over a stile in the stone wall in front, across the next field to another stile, after which you join a clear, winding track. Where the track ends (at a field gate in front), turn left through a gate to follow a grassy path by the side of a plantation. At the next gate turn left along the edge of a field and, where the plantation ends, walk along by the wall on the left, go through a gate and continue across the next field. About half-way across turn left through a gate and immediately right to continue by a wall on the right.

Go through the gate ahead, carry on with a hedge to your right and, at the corner of a wall, go straight ahead across the middle of the field. Just before the far end, bear right through a gate, turn left (by a hedge and fence on the left) and at the end of the field climb a fence and cross a stream (arrow waymark). Walk across the next field drawing towards the wooded valley on the right and making for the far right-hand corner, where you go through a gate. Below is the River Cover and you keep straight, parallel to the river, joining a wire fence on the left until you see a bridge over the river below. Bear right to cross the bridge and continue uphill by a wall on the right, across the open expanses of Middleham Moor. At the road turn right and follow the wide verge at the side of the road. You soon get a good view of the houses and castle of Middleham ahead, and you follow the road into the small town.

Middleham Castle

The grim ruined walls of Middleham Castle dominate the attractive, small, grey stone town with its two squares. It has a basically simple design; a huge Norman keep, built in 1170, surrounded by a 13th century curtain wall with a gatehouse in the south-east corner. The keep is one of the largest in the country - 105 x 78 feet with walls 10-12 feet thick. Despite its forbidding appearance, it was a residence as well as a fortress and contained cellars, kitchen, great hall, chapel and living quarters.

For two centuries the castle was owned by the powerful Neville family, the earls of Warwick. Probably the best known member of the family was Richard Neville, 'Warwick the King maker', who played a leading role in the Wars of the Roses. At first he supported the Yorkist cause but later switched to the Lancastrians. After his death at the Battle of Barnet (1471) the castle was forfeited to the Crown and the Yorkist king Edward IV gave it to his brother, Richard of Gloucester, who later became Richard III. Whether his reputation as one of the most evil monarchs in English history is justified or not is debatable, but after his death at Bosworth in 1485, Middleham Castle was taken over by the victor and his successor, Henry VII, and remained in royal hands until sold in 1604. Like most English castles it was 'slighted', i.e. destroyed to the extent that it could not be used again, on Cromwell's

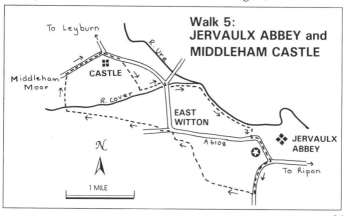

orders after the Civil War.

Route Directions (Middleham Castle to Jervaulx Abbey)

From the centre of Middleham take the main road towards Ripon and, after 0.5 mile, bear half-right along a clear, straight, walled track. The mound in the field on the right is all that is left of the 11th century motte and bailey fortification; immediate predecessor of the present castle.

The broad track later becomes a narrow path, and where it ends you go through the metal gate and continue by the edge of a field down to the River Cover. Turn left and follow the riverbank, crossing three stiles (yellow arrow waymarks), eventually bearing left to the main road. Turn right over the bridge and immediately left to follow the other bank of the Cover. Soon you reach the confluence of the Cover and Ure and the remainder of the walk (about 1.5 miles) is along a broad, grassy and very attractive path on the banks of the Ure with grand views across the fields all the way. Just before reaching Jervaulx Hall the path swings to the right away from the river, through a gate and up to the road. Turn left past Jervaulx Hall and follow the road for the short distance to the abbey entrance.

Jervaulx Abbey

Jervaulx is no Fountains or Bolton; compared with them its ruins are fragmentary but what it lacks in substance, it makes up for in atmosphere and a superb, tranquil location. Its history seems to have been uneventful. If was founded by the Cistercians in 1158 and, like most of the monasteries of Yorkshire, grew wealthy from the proceeds of sheep farming. In addition the monks of Jervaulx made cheese and bred horses, thereby creating both the Wensleydale cheese industry, and the local racehorse connections, (based at Middleham). The most eventful episode in the abbey's history was its closure, on Henry VIII's orders, in 1536. The last abbot, Adam of Sedbergh, took part in the Pilgrimage of Grace, a northern-based rebellion against the dissolution of the monasteries, and suffered the same fate in 1537 as his contemporary, John Paslew, at Whalley - execution.

It is a sign of the abbey's wealth that the church was 270 feet long, but little is left of it now apart from a fine Norman doorway and the bases of the pillars. Substantial portions of the domestic buildings around the cloister survive, notably the chapter house with its three Norman arches, kitchen, monk's dormitory and infirmary. Most of the buildings date from the 12th and 13th centuries.

The apparent random jumble of ruined walls may appear confusing, but it is enjoyable just to wander round Jervaulx, soaking up the atmosphere without getting too academic about what belongs where and what this particular building was used for. Apart from being incredibly peaceful, the absence of neatly trimmed lawns and notice-boards and the presence of climbing plants all over the walls, make the ruins seem more authentic - just what a ruined medieval abbey should look like.

Bolton Priory occupies a beautiful position by the River Wharfe

6. BOLTON PRIORY AND BARDEN TOWER

Start and Finish: Bolton Abbey
Distance: 8 miles   *Approximate Time:* 4 hours
Ordnance Survey Landranger Map: 104
Parking: Bolton Abbey
Refreshments: Bolton Abbey, Barden Tower and Cavendish Pavilion
Cafe.

General Description
Combine the picturesque ruins of a medieval monastery and hunting
lodge with the unrivalled scenery of the Yorkshire Dales, and the result
is a superb walk of great beauty and variety. The outward journey is
across fields and over moorland, with glorious views of Wharfedale,
and the return is along the banks of the Wharfe, by river meadows and
woodland, passing through the spectacular rocky gorge of the Strid.

Route Directions (Bolton Priory to Barden Tower)
From Bolton Abbey car park take the road to Burnsall for a short way
and soon after passing under an arch, bear half-left on to a track
signposted to Halton East. The path is very easy to follow as it is

waymarked with blue signs. Go through a gate and head straight across the field to a signpost near a wire fence, by the side of a pond. Follow the fence, go through a gate and turn right to cross a field and enter a wood. In a short while take a sharp left turn and follow the blue arrows through the wood, emerging at a gate in a stone wall. Now you are in open country and there are glorious panoramic views over Wharfedale to the right where Barden Tower can soon be seen down in the valley.

Following a line of blue stones across two large fields, go through a gate and then along a path that runs parallel to a wall on the left. The path now skirts a hill on the right and goes over the shoulder of the hill, bearing slightly to the right. Continue following the blue signs to a gate in the wall and keep on the track ahead to the road. Turn right and walk along the road for about 1.25 miles to a T-junction. Turn left and Barden Tower is just ahead.

Barden Tower
Barden Tower was a hunting lodge owned by the Cliffords of nearby Skipton Castle, one of the six such lodges in the old Forest of Barden. It was originally built in the 12th century but was rebuilt and considerably extended in the late 15th century by the tenth Lord Clifford. He was nicknamed the 'Shepherd Lord' as he preferred the quiet rural life here to the bustle of Skipton, and made Barden his chief residence. After his death in 1523 it was neglected and fell into ruin, but in the 17th

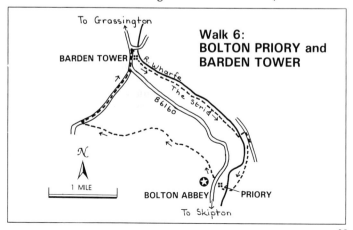

century it was restored by Lady Anne Clifford, who seems to have devoted most of her life and vast sums of money to restoring her various family properties, which included the castles of Brough, Brougham, Pendragon and Appleby in Cumbria as well as Skipton and Barden. During the late 18th and 19th centuries it was again abandoned and hence fell into ruin once more.

Although only a hunting lodge, Barden Tower looks as solid and powerful as a castle, occupying a fine position high above a wooded reach of the Wharfe. As well as being a place of residence it was also used for the administration of the forest laws, and from time to time as a refuge against marauding Scots which explains its fortress-like appearance. Separate from the main block is the former chapel and priest's house, part of the Shepherd Lord's 15th century extension, now a most attractive restaurant where you can relax in truly historic surroundings.

Route Directions (Barden Tower to Bolton Priory)

Follow the road past Barden Tower down to Barden Bridge. Just before the bridge go through a gap in the wall on the right, down some steps, and follow the west bank of the Wharfe through woodland and across meadows. The 3 mile walk from here to Bolton Abbey must be one of the loveliest riverside walks to be found anywhere in the country.

Go over two stiles, under a turreted bridge, across a meadow and through a gate to enter the Strid Woods. These woods are owned by the Devonshire Estates and a small charge is made for access to them. There are several paths through the woods marked with different coloured posts to denote various nature trails devised by the Devonshire Estates, but it is probably best to stick to the path closest to the river. However, in wet weather it can be quite slippery and dangerous, and in these conditions one of the alternative paths can be followed. Eventually you reach the Strid itself, where the river is only a few yards wide, and a very impressive sight it makes, surging over the rocks as it squeezes through the narrow gorge.

Past the Strid the riverside path broadens out onto a flat well-defined track. At a junction of paths bear slightly to the right, following the wider track uphill. The path soon drops down to the Cavendish Pavilion Cafe where you cross the footbridge, turn right and now follow the east bank of the river. Go through a stile in a stone wall, turn left by the stream, cross the road and then cross the stream by a footbridge. Follow the road uphill for a few yards and then bear right along a footpath signposted to Bolton Priory. Follow the path as it winds around through the trees giving glorious views of the great bend in the Wharfe and the priory ruins on the opposite bank. Eventually the paths drops down to a footbridge which you cross to gain access to the priory.

Bolton Priory

Although a priory, the monastery here is nearly always incorrectly referred to as an abbey and the adjacent village is called Bolton Abbey. Nevertheless this was always a priory served by Augustinian canons and was founded in 1154. Originally the Augustinians were given land on the nearby moors but they moved down here for shelter and a water supply and chose what is generally considered to be one of the most beautiful situations for any monastery in the country. Many writers and artists throughout the ages have enthused over the combination found here of the work of nature with the work of man, the priory harmonising perfectly with the composition of meadow, woodland, moorland and the sweep of the river.

Bolton Priory was built in the late 12th and 13 centuries, but the east end had to be rebuilt in the 14th century after the monastery had been raided and burnt by a Scottish army. Only twenty years before the priory was dissolved by Henry VIII and Thomas Cromwell in 1539, Prior Moone began the construction of a new west front and western tower but these were never completed. After the dissolution, the priory buildings and lands passed through several private hands and nowadays belong to the dukes of Devonshire.

The nave of the church has always been used as the local parish church and therefore has survived intact and is still used today. It is unusual in that it has two west fronts, the original 13th century one with the unfinished 16th century one built on to it. Presumably if the latter had ever been completed the earlier one would have been pulled down. Inside the church, which only has one aisle on the north side, there is a model of what the priory would have been like before the dissolution. The ruined east end of the church is dominated by the great east window, now open to the sky and offering views of the hills beyond. Apart from the church there is little else to see as the cloisters and surrounding domestic buildings have almost entirely disappeared. It is the magnificent setting rather than the buildings themselves that is the magnetic attraction at Bolton Priory.

The extensive ruins of Furness Abbey

7. FURNESS ABBEY AND PIEL CASTLE

Start: Furness Abbey   *Finish:* Roa Island
Distance: 6 miles   *Approximate Time:* 3 hours
Ordnance Survey Landranger Map: 96
Parking: Furness Abbey
Refreshments: Abbey Tavern by the abbey, Concle Inn at Rampside, pub and cafe at Roa Island, Ship Inn on Piel Island.

General Description

In the Middle Ages the abbots of Furness were virtual monarchs of this far-flung peninsula and the walk links the ruins of their great monastery with their castle on Piel Island, built to protect the coast from Scottish raids and approachable only by boat. Between the two you see plenty of evidence of the varied history of the area - peaceful farmland and coastal villages, abandoned iron mines and docks, Barrow ship-yards, and a power station and an onshore gas terminal, the latest development in the long industrial heritage of Furness that was largely started by the monks.

Furness Abbey

In 1127 monks of the Savignac Order established a monastery on the remote Furness peninsula, at that time a debatable and unsettled frontier region between England and Scotland, on land provided by Count Stephen of Boulogne and Mortain, later King of England. Here, in the deep Vale of Deadly Nightshade, arose one of the greatest and wealthiest monasteries in England. At the height of its power it was second only to Fountains among Cistercian abbeys (the Savignacs amalgamated with the Cistercians in 1147) and because of its relative inaccessibility its abbots wielded the power almost of independent monarchs.

The abbey's wealth was based on the acquisition and exploitation of vast amounts of land. At one time it owned 55,000 acres, which included most of Furness and estates throughout Cumbria, Lancashire and Yorkshire. It was the monks of Furness who initiated the clearing of the forests and began the large scale development of sheep farming, quarrying and iron mining, thus laying the foundation for the future growth of Barrow. In addition Furness Abbey had a large number of 'daugher monasteries' in England, the Isle of Man and Ireland and traded extensively, especially across the Irish Sea. The only setbacks to such capitalist enterprise were Scottish raids. There were two particularly serious ones in 1316, and 1322, and after the latter Robert the Bruce had the effrontery, not only to accept the bribes the abbot gave him to refrain from looting and destruction, but to continue to indulge in such activities on a large scale. It was after that incident that Piel Castle was built.

The well preserved and extensive ruins reflect the wealth and power of Furness Abbey. The church, 275 feet long, and the domestic buildings belong mostly to the second half of the 12th century and are built in the Transitional style, when the heavy, rounded Norman arches were giving way to the lighter, pointed Gothic ones. In the 13th century the cloisters were extended, the superb infirmary block was built in the 14th century, the east end of the church rebuilt in the 15th century and the western tower added around 1500. The transepts and east end of the church are virtually complete, as is the east range of the cloisters, noted for its flamboyant, decorative Norman arches leading into the 13th century chapter house.

Built of rich red local sandstone that glows in the sunlight and standing in a beautiful wooded setting, the ruins are among the most strikingly attractive in the country as well as being of immense architectural and historical interest. In such a green and tranquil environment it is difficult to believe that the industries of Barrow lie just over the hill in the next valley.

Route Directions
From the car park take the lane by the side of the abbey ruins round to the left past another car park, and uphill. Just after crossing a stream turn right on to a path (public footpath sign to Parkhouse Road), cross the railway line and continue ahead to a kissing gate. Go through and bear right along the edge of the field, shortly joining the stream on your right. Follow the bank of the stream up to a footbridge, cross over and follow the other bank up to the picturesque 15th century Bow Bridge, one of the links in the large number of pack-horse trails that radiated from the abbey prior to its dissolution in 1537.

Re-cross the stream at the bridge and turn left along the road to a crossroads. Here you go right through a kissing gate and walk straight ahead, uphill across a field climbing quite steeply. At the top of the hill (just before reaching another kissing gate and the houses of Newton), turn right along a grassy path parallel to a hedge and fence on the left, and make for a ladder-stile about 100 yards in front. Climb over and continue, bearing slightly left uphill across a field containing the remains of abandoned iron mines. Just before the top of the hill ahead look out for a stile in the fence on the left which you have to climb. However a detour of a few yards to the top of the hill rewards you with a panoramic view over much of Furness - the abbey ruins, farmland, Barrow docks and shipyards, iron mines, railway, Roosecote power station, Walney Island, Morecambe Bay coast and a glimpse of your destination, Piel Castle on its island in Walney Channel. This single view encapsulates much of the medieval and modern history of Furness - the abbey and castle dominating the Middle Ages and the iron mines, railway and shelter afforded by Walney Channel creating the basis for the 19th century industrial growth in the area.

After climbing the stile, bear slightly to the right and head in a straight line diagonally across the field, making for a kissing gate by a section of fencing in the hedge in front. Go through and turn right along a lane for the next 1.5 miles, through the romantically named farming hamlet of Stank and straight on at a crossroads along what is now called Dungeon Lane to the main A587 (Furness coast road) opposite Roosecote power station. Turn right along the road (wide verges both sides) and immediately before the road bears right by the

Barrow signpost, turn left along a path signposted to Salthouse Pool. Walk uphill along the edge of the field and over the brow, bear left away from the fence towards an electricity pylon. At the bottom end of the field turn right over a stile and almost immediately sharp left to join a wide, straight track, once the route of the Furness Railway and now converted to form part of the Cumbrian Coastal Way.

For the next 1.75 miles you keep along this track, passing in front of the power station and follow it around the promontory of Westfield Point in front of the onshore gas terminal, the latest development in Furness's industrial history, which receives gas from the Morecambe Bay field 40 miles out to sea. From Westfield Point there are fine views

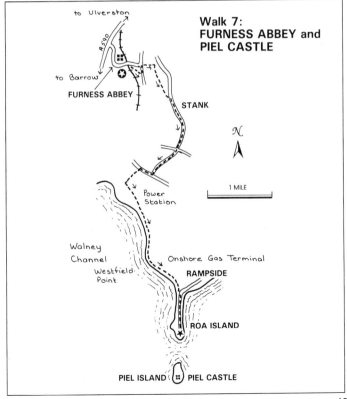

to Ulverston

A590

to Barrow

FURNESS ABBEY

Walk 7:
FURNESS ABBEY and PIEL CASTLE

STANK

N

1 MILE

Power Station

Walney Channel

Onshore Gas Terminal

Westfield Point

RAMPSIDE

ROA ISLAND

PIEL ISLAND PIEL CASTLE

45

across the channel to the flat expanses of Walney Island, and Piel Castle is clearly in sight all the way.

Continue along the track and, where it bears left, you have the choice of either following it inland or keeping straight on by the edge of the low cliffs to the village of Rampside. Here you walk along the causeway constructed by John Abel Smith in 1842 to connect Roa Island with the mainland. He also built a pier on the small island and a rail link in order to develop it as the main port for the booming Furness iron industry, but the development of Barrow ended that dream.

From the jetty at the far end of Roa Island a ferry takes you across to Piel Island, making a uniquely relaxing finale to this walk.

Piel Castle

The gaunt 14th century castle keep and its curtain walls still appropriately dominate the tiny island and the approaches to Walney Channel, which they were originally built to defend. Piel Island was part of the grant of land by Stephen to the monks of Furness Abbey and was used by them as a harbour. The castle was not built until the early 14th century when, after the two Scottish raids in 1316 and 1322, the abbot decided that his harbour and lucrative trade needed protection, not just from Scottish raiders but also from pirates in the Irish Sea. Over the next century it served as a sort of fortified warehouse, engaged in profitable smuggling as well as more legitimate trade, but for some unknown reason it seems to have been abandoned by the monks in the early 15th century.

Only once did this remote spot figure in an event of national importance. This was in 1487 when the pretender Lambert Simnel landed here after being crowned in Dublin, to claim the throne from Henry VII. His campaign ended in disaster a few months later on the battlefield of Stoke in Nottinghamshire.

After the dissolution of the abbey the island passed to the Crown and the castle was left to fall gradually into decay. The harbour remained in use until the 19th century rise of Barrow.

There is an infrequent bus service from Roa Island to Barrow town centre, and a much more frequent service from Barrow town centre which drops you a short distance from Furness Abbey. Details of these and information about ferries to Piel Island are available from Barrow Tourist Information Office (0229 25795).

*The Norman Keep of Clitheroe Castle - small
but still dominates the Ribble valley*

8. WHALLEY ABBEY AND CLITHEROE CASTLE

Start: Whalley *Finish:* Clitheroe
Distance: 6 miles   *Approximate Time:* 3 hours
Ordnance Survey Landranger Map: 103
Parking: Whalley and Clitheroe
Refreshments: Pubs and cafes in Whalley and Clitheroe, Wellsprings
Inn at the Nick of Pendle, Swan with Two Necks in Pendleton.

General Description
An invigorating walk of great variety across fields, by woodland and
over open and rugged moorland, with fine views over the Ribble and
Calder valleys, linking the two principal medieval ruins in Lancashire,
one ecclesiastical and the other military.

Whalley Abbey
The abbey is situated on the banks of the River Calder very close to the
church and village centre, and is clearly signposted. It was founded in

1283 by Cistercian monks who moved here from Stanlow on the River Mersey (the site of which is now surrounded by power stations and chemical works) because of frequent flooding. The land was provided by the powerful Henry de Lacy from nearby Clitheroe Castle who also owned the site at Stanlow and was keen to help the monks in their search for new premises.

The buildings were constructed mainly in the 14th century, apart from the fine north-east gateway through which you enter, which was completed around 1480. Whalley was a fairly small monastery; at its height it only housed about 30 monks and towards the end considerably fewer than that. It was dissolved by Henry VIII in 1536 and the last abbot, John Paslew, was hanged at Lancaster Castle the following year for sheltering rebels during the Pilgrimage of Grace, a revolt that spread throughout much of the north of England against the closure of the monasteries. After the dissolution the monastic buildings and grounds passed to the Assheton family, who built the Elizabethan mansion that is now used as a conference centre by the diocese of Blackburn.

Of the church only the foundations are left, but there are quite considerable remains of the cloisters and domestic buildings. The most complete building is the cellarium and lay brothers' dormitory on the west side of the cloisters, but this is used by the Roman Catholic church as a hall and is not normally open to the public. Particularly imposing are the two gateways. The north-east one serves as the main entrance to the site, and the stone-vaulted 14th century north-west gateway lies outside the abbey precincts astride a lane called The Sands.

Route Directions (Whalley Abbey to Clitheroe Castle)
From the abbey walk along Church Street, past the medieval parish church, to the main road. Turn left and opposite Mitton Road turn right along Brookes Lane. At the end go through a gate and follow the path by the edge of a stream. Climb a stile and continue uphill along a clear grassy path, parallel to a line of trees on the left, bearing slightly right to climb another stile. Turn right through the trees to reach the road opposite Spring Wood, a popular picnic area.

Cross the road and just past the traffic lights, turn left through a gap into the grounds of Whalley Golf Club. Continue uphill keeping to the edge of the golf course by the side of Spring Wood. Climb a stile and cross a footbridge on the left near some trees, turn right and continue uphill. At this stage you may feel like a short rest to admire the glorious view behind over Whalley Nab and the Calder Valley. Keep close to a wire fence on the left, climb a stile in that fence at the top end of the field, turn right to climb another stile a few yards ahead and right again, over another stile and follow the wall on the right around the back of a large house. At the end of the buildings bear right through a gate and turn left along a wide track. In about 50 yards you come to a road where you turn left.

You will be pleased to know that the uphill part of the walk is virtually over. After a while the road peters out and becomes a clearly defined track which you follow almost in a straight line for about 2 miles across breezy and open moorland. There are superb views over

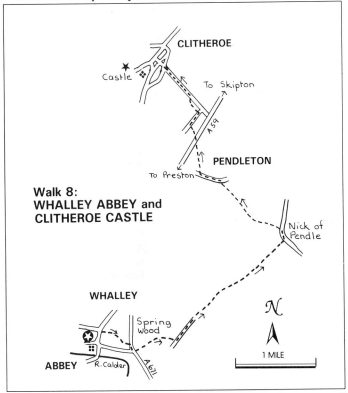

Wiswell Moor to the left, the slopes of Pendle Hill in front, and to the right the village of Sabden in its wooded valley, with glimpses of industrial Lancashire on the horizon.

Eventually you come out on to the Clitheroe-Sabden road where you turn left and follow the road up to the Nick of Pendle. At the top, where the road veers to the right down to the Wellsprings Hotel, turn left through a gate and follow the path down to a stone wall. In front of you is a fine panoramic view across the Ribble Valley, with the town and castle of Clitheroe clearly visible in the distance. At the wall climb a stile and continue downhill along a clearly defined path. Look out for a stile in the wall on the right, climb it and head down towards some farm buildings keeping to their right-hand side. Go through a gap in the wall ahead and continue down to a stile. Turn right over it, proceed to another stile ahead which you climb and then turn sharp left downhill. At the bottom cross a footbridge, bear left and follow the grassy path down into the village of Pendleton.

Walk through the village and at the end of the village street follow the track ahead (public footpath sign to Clitheroe). Climb a stone wall, continue for a few yards and then bear right and head diagonally across the field to a footbridge. Cross over and head across the next field to another footbridge, cross and continue over the next field to a stile in the fence. Climb over, turn right and then left at the farm track to cross the Whalley-Clitheroe bypass. Carry on over a stile, bear right and head diagonally across a field. Cross a footbridge and walk across the next field to a stile which brings you out onto a lane.

Turn right for about 100 yards and, opposite a cottage, turn left over a stile and walk along the edge of a field. Climb a stile, bear right and follow the path across the next field to the road. Turn left and follow the road down into the centre of Clitheroe where the castle is clearly visible.

Clitheroe Castle

The castle grounds are now a municipal park owned by the Ribble Valley Borough Council. You enter them at the top of Castle Street in order to make your way up to the early 12th century keep, which claims to be the smallest Norman keep in the country, though this is disputed by Goodrich in the Wye Valley.

Clitheroe Castle was founded around 1080 by Roger de Poitou, who was given extensive estates between the Mersey and the Ribble (the 'Honour of Clitheroe') by William the Conqueror as a reward for helping him gain the English throne at the battle of Hastings. In 1102 it passed to the de Lacy family and the present remains are of Robert de Lacy's early 12th century building. Later the castle passed into the possession of the House of Lancaster, and ultimately the Crown.

Despite its small size it was a strong castle, occupying a natural defensive position and commanding the Ribble Valley. The keep makes a fine vantage point with extensive views over Pendle Hill and the Bowland Fells. Throughout its long history Clitheroe Castle saw little action, though in the Civil War between Charles I and Parliament it was attacked and captured from the Parliamentarians by the King's nephew and cavalry leader, Prince Rupert, in 1644. A few year later it was slighted on the orders of Oliver Cromwell and today there is little left apart from the keep. The other buildings, one of which houses the Castle Museum, are mostly 18th century reconstructions.

In order to get back to your starting point use the regular bus service between Clitheroe and Whalley. Details from Clitheroe Tourist Information Office (0200 25566).

Cartmel Priory from the south

9. CARTMEL PRIORY AND HOLKER HALL

Start and Finish: Cartmel
Distance: 6.5 miles   *Approximate Time:* 3hrs 30mins
Ordnance Survey Landranger Map: 97
Parking: Cartmel
Refreshments: Pubs and cafes in Cartmel, restaurant at Holker Hall.

General Description
This is a most attractive circular walk around the picturesque monastic village of Cartmel mainly along farm tracks, quiet winding lanes and fellside paths. For most of the route the tower of Cartmel Priory is visible and the advantages of walking in this quiet rolling country, on the southern fringes of the Lake District between the mountains and the sea, are the superb panoramic views over both Morecambe Bay and the Cumbrian mountains, especially from the summit of the 727 feet high Hampsfield Fell.

Route Directions (Cartmel Priory to Holker Hall)
From the village square in Cartmel (near the 14th century priory

gatehouse), take the lane to the left of the Post Office, past the village hall, through the car park of Cartmel racecourse and along the broad track that curves to the left across one corner of the racecourse. The route to Holker (about 1.5 miles) is easy to follow as it is a straight, clear track all the way.

Go through three gates, entering woodland after the last one. Continue through the wood to go through a gate at the far end, and where the track forks take the uphill one on the right. You soon get a fine view over Morecambe Bay. At a junction of tracks, go through the gate ahead (ignoring the parallel path through the woods), to follow the winding tarmac track down to the road. Turn left and the main gate to Holker Hall and park is just down the hill on the right.

Holker Hall
There are a number of links between Holker Hall and Cartmel Priory. Before the dissolution of the monasteries Holker was part of the priory estates, and since the dissolution two of the owners of Holker, George Preston in the early 17th century and the seventh Duke of Devonshire in the mid-19th century, have been responsible for carrying out restorations of the priory church.

The Prestons, a local family, were the first owners of the estate and George Preston built the original house in the early 17th century. The lack of male heirs meant the estate passed by marriage to the Lowthers in 1697 and then to the Cavendishes in 1756. The latter were one of the

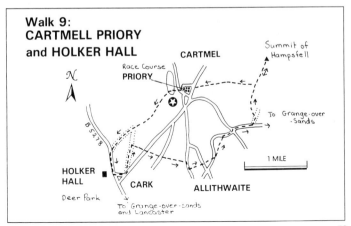

Walk 9:
CARTMELL PRIORY
and HOLKER HALL

most powerful and wealthy families in England at the time, holders of the title of Dukes of Devonshire, and thus Holker became part of the vast Devonshire estates that embraced, amongst others, Chatsworth in Derbyshire and Bolton Abbey in North Yorkshire. Indeed it was the favourite residence of the seventh Duke who even preferred it to the more palatial Chatsworth House.

Little is left of George Preston's original structure and the present house is basically a grand Victorian mansion comprising the New Wing, totally rebuilt in the Elizabethan style after a fire in 1871, and the Old Wing, an 18th century construction with 19th century additions and ornamentation. The Old Wing is private and visitors tour only the New Wing, an outstanding example of an ornate, late 19th century country house, one of the last to be built before a combination of changing social patterns and high taxation made such places impractical.

Inside, the main rooms include the superb library, the dining room, bedrooms and dressing rooms, the hall and the splendid long gallery. All contain fine furniture, pictures, panelling and some exceptionally elaborate fireplaces. From the windows there are views over the attractive formal gardens and landscaped deer park, mostly laid out in the 18th and 19th centuries.

Apart from the house and grounds, Holker Hall's other attractions include a motor museum, craft and countryside museum and adventure playground for children.

Route Directions (Holker Hall to Cartmel Priory)
On leaving the park entrance turn right and walk along the road towards Cark. Where the main road bends to the right at the 'Rose and Crown' carry on (signposted Cartmel and Newby Bridge) along a minor road. Keep left at the road junction and, just past a derestriction sign, turn left through a metal gate and follow a tarmac track which curves uphill to the right giving fine views over the valley of the winding River Ea, with the fells in the background and the tower of Cartmel Priory in front. Pass through a gate and walk along a rougher track to a farm, where you turn right to follow a track down to the river and road.

Go straight across the road, over some steps in the wall opposite (public footpath sign to Templands via Birkby Hall) and proceed uphill across the field, gradually bearing away from the hedge and wall on the left to climb a ladder-stile in the wall ahead. Continue across the next field (wall on the right), cross a lane and carry on along a drive (public footpath sign to Allithwaite) that leads up to two large houses. The one on the right is Birkby Hall. Follow the footpath directions along the side and back of the house on the left and around the edge of the garden, then take the path on the right that heads uphill through a belt of trees. Climb the steps ahead and continue uphill across the middle of the field making for a stile by a gate. Climb over and carry on heading towards some farm buildings. At this point there are grand views over Morecambe Bay in front and the Lakeland fells to the left. Look out for a stile on the left (near a gate and separating the hedge from the wall), climb over and walk along the edge of the field (hedge on right) to the lane. Turn right and about 100 yards ahead, near some houses, turn left along a tarmac track where there is a public footpath sign to Grange and Lindale.

With the houses on the edge of Allithwaite on your right, walk along the track to a lane, cross over and carry on along the edge of the field opposite, squeezing through a narrow gap in the wall ahead, continue to the next lane where you turn left. You turn right shortly, through a wooden gate, to head uphill across rough pastureland, at first keeping parallel with the lane below on the left but gradually bearing away from it. At the brow of the hill make for the right-hand side of the line of houses in front and climb some steps in the wall ahead to rejoin the lane. Turn right and follow it as it curves left up to a crossroads. Continue straight on along Grange Fell Road (signposted Grange-over-Sands Town Centre) and, just past a golf club on the left, turn left along a narrow uphill lane.

Ignoring a public footpath sign to Cartmel on the left, carry on along the lane, pausing to admire the superb view on the right over the Kent estuary, Arnside Knott, Silverdale and the long line of the Pennines in the background. From now on the views get better and better as you approach the summit of Hampsfield Fell. Where you see a public footpath sign on the right to Ashmount Road and Charney Road, turn left through a gate and take the path ahead. Follow it as it curves right and continue along the distinct grassy path that you can see stretching ahead in a straight line across the fell, cutting a swathe through the fern and bracken as it heads for the top. Climb a stile in the wall ahead and carry on climbing steadily all the while. At a crossroads of green tracks (near a telegraph pole) you can turn left to Cartmel, but the extra 0.75 mile return trip from this point to the summit of Hampsfield Fell (727 feet) is worth the extra effort for the magnificent view. If you decide to press ahead to the top, continue along the track and soon you will see the hospice (stone hut with an observation platform) that marks the summit. The panoramic view from it must rank as one of the finest as it takes in the whole sweep of Morecambe Bay, Kent estuary, Pennines and Lakeland mountains.

If the weather is fine and the conditions clear it will be with some reluctance that you drag yourself away to retrace your steps to the crossroads of tracks. There you turn right and follow the clear grassy path as it heads downhill, keeping roughly parallel with a line of telegraph poles on the right, with views of Cartmel Priory in front all the way. Go through a metal gate and walk across the field ahead, bearing slightly away from the wall on the right to go through a gate. Continue across the next field in the direction of some farm buildings and, keeping to the right of those buildings, go through a gate in the wall (signposted Cartmel) and carry on across the next field (hedge on left). At the road turn left and immediately right to the priory.

Cartmel Priory

The small Augustinian priory of Cartmel was founded in 1190 by William Marshall Earl of Pembroke, one of the most powerful barons of the time. It is likely that the village grew up around the priory because the area was very sparsely populated. Situated in such a remote spot far from the main lines of communication and major areas of turmoil, Cartmel Priory enjoyed a largely peaceful history until its dissolution in 1537, when some of its canons were executed for taking part of the Pilgrimage of Grace, a protest movement against Henry VIII's monastic closures.

Following the dissolution the domestic buildings were demolished - the stones no doubt serving as a convenient quarry for the local people - but the church survived because part of it, the south choir aisle or Town Choir, had been used as the parish church and was bought by the parishioners. The rest of the church was in a derelict state for over half a century until restored by George Preston of Holker in the early 17th century. A further period of neglect and decay was followed by a major restoration carried out by the seventh Duke of Devonshire in the 19th century.

From the outside the most distinguishing features are the large east window and the unusual design of the tower. When the tower was heightened in the 15th century the extension, for some unknown reason, was built diagonally to the original tower, giving it a highly distinctive and not unattractive appearance. Inside, the church is a mixture of styles. Most of the east end is Transitional Norman work of the late 12th century, belonging to the original church, the south choir aisle was built in the 14th century and the nave and east window date from the 15th century. The nave is plain and unusually short - only three bays - possibly an indication of the relative poverty of the Cartmel canons compared with their richer brethren at such monasteries as Fountains or nearby Furness. Look out particularly for the magnificent east window and the intricate carvings of the 15th century choir stalls with their elaborate 17th century screens. In the nave is a monument to Lord Frederick Cavendish, ambushed and brutally murdered in Phoenix Park Dublin, in 1882, soon after taking up his duties as Chief Secretary of Ireland.

Cartmel is unusual in that the cloisters and surrounding domestic buildings were originally built, as normal, on the south side of the church, but later in the 14th century rebuilt on the north side. The reason is not clear - among the suggested explanations are fire, Scottish raids or marshy ground.

Nothing remains of them however, and the only building apart from the church to survive the dissolution is the 14th century gatehouse, now forming an entrance to the village square and once used as a schoolroom.

The magnificent ruins of Fountains Abbey

10. FOUNTAINS ABBEY AND STUDLEY ROYAL COUNTRY PARK

Start and Finish: Fountains Abbey
Distance: 4.5 miles   *Approximate Time:* 2 hours
Ordnance Survey Landranger Map: 99
Parking: Fountains Abbey
Refreshments: Cafe at Fountains Abbey

General Description
The most spectacular and complete monastic ruins in Europe form the centrepiece of this unusually attractive and varied walk. The route goes across fields and through woodlands, a deer park and landscaped gardens and includes fine views over the surrounding countryside. It embraces in a short distance such diverse attractions as the 12th century abbey, 17th century hall, 18th century water gardens and a 19th century church.

Route Directions (Fountains Abbey to Studley Roger)
From the car park turn right along the road (signposted to Harrogate) and follow it as it curves uphill by the side of the boundary wall to the

58

abbey grounds. Just past a stream turn left over a stile (public footpath sign) on to a clear and well-defined path. The route is easy to follow and well waymarked, from it there is a fine view of Fountains Abbey and Hall down in the valley on the left. Go through two gates, follow the path around the right-hand side of a farm, continue along the edge of a field (hedge on right) and, where the hedge finishes, ignore the clear farm track ahead and bear left downhill to a gate near the edge of a wood.

Go through the gate and take the path through the wood, passing one of the entrances (ruined) to the Studley Royal Estate on the left. In front of you there are extensive views towards Ripon and over the Vale of York with the long line of the Hambleton Hills forming an impressive backcloth. Descend a hill and, at a crossroads of tracks, turn sharp left (ignoring the public footpath sign to Ripon) to continue downhil through a steep-sided wooded valley. At the bottom (near a ford), cross the footbridge over the River Skell, turn right and follow the broad track uphill. At the top of the ridge you leave the woods and emerge into open country with more fine views over to the right, the towers of Ripon Cathedral standing out clearly. Approaching the village of Studley Roger the rough track becomes surfaced. Just before the village you turn left to enter the Studley Royal Country Park.

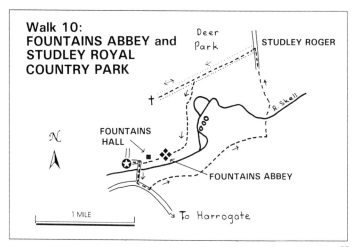

Walk 10:
FOUNTAINS ABBEY and
STUDLEY ROYAL
COUNTRY PARK

Deer Park

STUDLEY ROGER

R. Skell

FOUNTAINS HALL

𝒩

FOUNTAINS ABBEY

1 MILE

To Harrogate

Studley Royal Country Park

As you walk along the straight drive through the park, look back and you can see Ripon Cathedral aligned exactly with the drive; part of John Aislabie's grand scheme that envisaged Ripon Cathedral at one end of his park and Fountains Abbey at the other.

The deer park of Studley Royal was created in the 16th century but its present appearance dates mainly from 1699 when the estate came into the ownership of John Aislabie. He was an astute and wealthy man with grandiose ambitions who for a time was Chancellor of the Exchequer before being forced to resign, and even serving a brief spell of imprisonment in the Tower of London, because of his involvement in the financial scandal of 1720 known as the South Sea Bubble. Following this enforced retirement from public life, he directed his energies into transforming part of his estate into a splendid and unique landscaped water garden. The course of the River Skell was altered to create a series of lakes, canals and cascades. Embankments and hills were constructed, trees planted, and a number of imitation classical temples and other buildings erected, all linked to provide carefully planned vistas. John Aislabie wanted to make the ruins of Fountains Abbey the climax of his design, the ultimate in garden ornaments, but it was his son William who complete the dream by purchasing the neighbouring estate that included Fountains Abbey and Hall in 1768, for £18,000, and adding it to his existing property.

The fused estate of Studley Royal and Fountains has passed through several hands and in 1983 was bought by the National Trust. Since then the Trust has embarked upon an ambitious and expensive programme of restoration for both the grounds and the various ancillary buildings.

Route Directions (Studley Roger to Fountains Abbey)

From the Studley Roger entrance make your way along the drive, in line with the church spire and through the elegant 18th century gateway, to enter the deer park. You may well be lucky enough to see deer grazing in the rough grassland amid the random clumps of trees on the right.

At a junction of park roads, turn left down to the lakeside and restaurant, near where you pay to enter the landscaped gardens and abbey ruins. It is worthwhile first to continue ahead for a few hundred yards to take a look at the fine, ornate Victorian church built in the

1870's by the well-known architect William Burges.

After entering the landscaped gardens keep to the main path as it threads its way around the side of small lakes, canals and cascades, by classical temples, across lawns and through woods, finally following the riverbank to the abbey. The views are superb but the finest of all, as John Aislabie himself intended, is the first stunning view of the abbey ruins themselves.

Fountains Abbey

In 1132 a group of Benedictine monks, discontented with the lax standards at St. Mary's Abbey in York, moved to the remote and barren wilderness of Skelldale and, on land provided by the Archbishop of York, commenced the building of the Cistercian abbey of Fountains. From these small beginnings rose what was to become the greatest and wealthiest Cistercian monastery in England. At the height of its power in the 13th and 14th centuries Fountains Abbey owned vast areas of arable land and sheep pastures in Yorkshire, plus fisheries, lead mines and quarries. Its wealth and power did not save it from being dissolved by Henry VIII in 1539, but its comparative remoteness did ensure that its buildings remained almost intact.

A tour of the remains should start with the church, built in the late 12th century and 300 feet long. It is an outstanding example of the Transitional style of architecture and is virtually complete, apart from roof and windows. It has two particularly unusual features. First the east end, enlarged in the 13th century by the erection of the Chapel of the Nine Altars. This is a rectangular structure built sideways onto the church and extends beyond its width like an extra pair of transepts; the only other one of its kind in the country is at Durham Cathedral. Second, the 170 feet high tower, built by Abbot Huby in the late 15th century as a reflection of the abbey's prosperity, which rises above the north transept instead of, as usual, above the central tower.

The cloisters and surrounding buildings mostly belong to the 13th century and reflect the many facets of monastic life. They include places for business meetings, kitchens, dining halls, sleeping quarters, store houses, cellars, guest houses, and the private residence of the abbot. They are best explored using a ground plan. The finest building of all is the great stone-vaulted cellarium occupying the western range of the cloisters, it is over 300 feet long and in an excellent state of preservation. Its ground floor was used as a store room and dining hall for the lay brothers, and the upper floor (now disappeared) was the lay brothers' dormitory. Some of the buildings extended over the River Skell and were reached by several attractive medieval bridges. The river provided fresh water, fish and drainage facilities for the community.

The unusually complete nature of those monastic buildings gives us a vivid insight into the way of life of the monks, and clearly indicates that Fountains Abbey was not just a self-contained religious community, but also the centre of an extensive capitalist empire based on sheep farming and land ownership. Not what its original founders intended.

Leaving the abbey you pass Fountains Hall (on the right), a fine Jacobean mansion of the early 17th century built (partly of stones from the abbey), by Sir Richard Gresham, one of the inheritors of the monastic estates. Inside is an exhibition about the work of the National Trust and its future plans for the area, and there you can watch a film telling the story of Fountains Abbey and Studley Royal Park.

Bolton Castle - high up in Wensleydale and visible for miles around

11. BOLTON CASTLE

Start and Finish: Aysgarth
Distance: 7 miles *Approximate Time:* 3hrs 30mins
Ordnance Survey Landranger Map: 98
Parking: Aysgarth Falls
Refreshments: Cafes in Aysgarth, restaurant at Bolton Castle, Wheatsheaf at Carperby.

General Description
Starting and finishing at a spectacular series of waterfalls on the River Ure, this walk takes you across fields to the substantial ruins of Bolton Castle standing high up on the northern slopes of Wensleydale and visible for miles around. Expansive views are the main features of this walk and the ideal time to do it is on a fine day after rain, when the hills stand out clearly and the falls are in full spate.

Route Directions (Aysgarth to Bolton Castle)
Aysgarth Falls is a series of three falls strung out along a 0.75 mile stretch of the River Ure. The Upper Falls come first, you reach them by taking the signposted path at the far end of the car park. It winds

through woods, beside a short stretch of road and through a gate up to the side of the falls.

Returning to the gate, go through on to the road by the bridge, turn left and follow it for a short distance to a gate where there is a signpost to Middle and Lower Falls. Turn right and follow the woodland path to view the Middle Falls - a most impressive sight with the torrent of water backed by the tower of Aysgarth church on the hill behind. Continue along the woodland path, through a gate, across a meadow and through another gate, plunging down again into riverside woods to see the Lower Falls.

Soon afterwards you leave the river, and the rest of the route to Bolton Castle is easy to follow as there are signposts and yellow waymarks all the way. After walking along the riverside path for a few yards, turn left over a stile, head across the field towards a fence and turn right, keeping by the fence on your left. Where the fence ends go through a gap in the wall ahead, continue across the field in a straight line, veering slightly to the left to a gate. Go through and along the path to a farm, through a gate and turn right through the farmyard, passing the back of the farmhouse, to continue along a broad track. It is at this point that superb vistas up and down Wensleydale open up, including a clear view of Bolton Castle (which will be in sight for most of the rest of the way).

After a few yards you bear right away from the farm track, keeping by a wire fence on the right and heading straight in the direction of the castle. Approaching a wall on the right, turn right over some steps and continue across the middle of the field, making for a

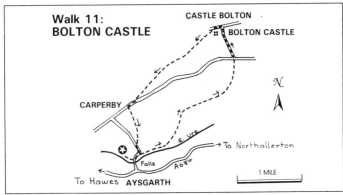

64

large group of farm buildings. On reaching a wall, bear right over a stile by a metal gate, carry on by the wall, over another stile, walk another few yards to a gap in the wall and on again by a wall on your right. At the corner of the wall, head towards another wall and a line of trees in front. Follow the path along the left-hand side of the wall, over a stile and then walk for the next 0.75 mile along a green lane lined with hedges for most of the way. This is an ancient routeway called Thoresby Lane and some mounds in a field on the right are all that remains of the Danish settlement of Thoresby, deserted sometime in the Middle Ages.

During this section of the walk you cross a beck and, near the end of the green lane, come to a farm. About 100 yards past the farmhouse, bear left off the track to cross a footbridge, turn left through a gap in the fence, carry on over a low stone wall and ignoring the ladder-stile in front, turn right by the side of the wall on your right. The wall soon ends but you keep straight on towards a barn at the far end of the field. Go through a gap in the wall to the right of the barn and walk straight across the field, in the direction of the castle, to a gap in the wall alongside a metal gate. This brings you out on to the road which you follow for 0.5 mile (ahead) up to the village of Castle Bolton and the castle itself.

Bolton Castle

Bolton Castle is somewhat misleading. As you approach it up the hill the high walls look almost impenetrable, and a superficial tour of the ruins suggests that they are every schoolboys dream of what a medieval castle should be - mysterious nooks and crannies, narrow passages and stairways, dark corners and, of course, the essential dungeon: a suitably small, grim room which prisoners unceremoniously entered by being dropped through the gap in the roof.

In reality, however, Bolton was built for residential as much as military reasons and its outer walls protected mostly domestic buildings. It was one of the later medieval castles, built towards the end of the 14th century by Sir Richard le Scrope, Lord Chancellor to Richard II who gave him the licence to crenellate (i.e fortify) his manor house at Bolton in 1379. There is no powerful keep or strongly guarded gatehouse, but simply rectangular walls three storeys high with a five storey tower in each of the four corners. All the buildings are grouped around the curtain walls, thus leaving an open courtyard in the middle though, because of the height of the walls, it is somewhat gloomy and almost permanently sunless. On the ground floor the buildings are chiefly storehouses, stables, bakehouse and brewery while the kitchens and living quarters, including the chapel, are on the first and second floors.

The castle served as one of the many prisons occupied by Mary Queen of Scots during her nineteen years of captivity in England at the hands of Elizabeth I. She was only here for a short time - less than a year, from July 1568 to January 1569 - and the room on the second floor of the south-west tower, now called Mary's Room, is unlikely to be the one she used during her period of imprisonment. During the Civil War between Charles and Parliament the castle suffered a year long siege before being captured by the Parliamentary army in 1645, and shortly afterwards slighted on Cromwell's orders. Today it must be virtually unique as a medieval ruin in having a bar and restaurant in the north-west tower - very conveniently sited at about the half-way stage of the walk.

The small one-street village, really no more than a hamlet, and tiny church lie huddled beneath and are dwarfed by the castle's high walls. They are a vivid illustration of the insecurity of life in the Middle Ages.

Route Directions (Bolton Castle to Aysgarth)
Take the tarmac lane past the castle, on past the car park, over a stile and into a field. Bearing left, make for a stile near the corner of a wall (yellow waymarks) climb over and proceed to another stile. Climb over that and keep on to the end of the wall where you bear left across the middle of the field, heading gradually downhill towards two metal gates side by side. At this point there are more marvellous views across Wensleydale, with the castle still a prominent landmark behind.

Go through the lower gate and walk across the field, keeping roughly parallel with the fence and wall on the right, before veering left to a stile next to a gate in the wall ahead. Climb over and keep on to cross a footbridge, bear half-right uphill to a wall, go left through a gap and continue to a metal gate in the wall ahead. Go through and head towards the farm in front, pass the left-hand side of the farm buildings, and walk on for a few yards along the farm track. At a public footpath sign bear right through a gap in the wall, keep straight on to the next gap, go through and follow the wall of a plantation on the left to a stile.

Climb over and continue, bearing left to cross a stream, and then slightly right (with the stream on your right) to a gate in a wall. Go through and walk along a grassy path (parallel to a fence on the right), through a metal gate and straight ahead across the next field to a gap in the wall. Go through and (wire fence on the right) cross the field, which contains a number of prominent mounds, to pick up a track which veers left downhill, through a gate and on through a farmyard to a road. Turn right and follow the road into the village of Carperby.

At the Wheatsheaf turn left through a gate (public footpath sign) into a narrow field, cross a small stream and, a few yards further on, go right through a metal gate. Turn left immediately and follow a straight path (wall on the left) across several fields and through a gate to a lane. Cross over and take the path opposite across a field (wall on the right). Go right through a gap in the wall at a public footpath sign, bear half-left and follow the path diagonally across four fields and through four gaps in walls. After the fourth gap, you enter a small wood where you bear right at a path junction and then immediately left, down through the wood and through a gate on to a road. Turn left under the bridge and first right back to Aysgarth Falls car park.

Arnside Tower - built to guard Morecambe Bay from Scottish Raiders

12. ARNSIDE TOWER

Start and Finish: Arnside
Distance: 6 miles   *Approximate Time:* 3 hours
Ordnance Survey Landranger Map: 97
Parking: Promenade at Arnside
Refreshments: Pubs and cafes in Arnside

General Description
It would be difficult to conceive a short walk with greater variety and
more splendid scenery than this one. Based on the small resort of
Arnside it includes open hillside, some lovely stretches of woodland,
low cliffs, sea marshes, a river estuary and passes a picturesque ruined
pele tower. The climb to the summit of the modest 522 feet Arnside
Knott is rewarded with superb panoramic views that encompass the
Furness Fells, Lakeland mountains, Pennines and the broad sweep of
Morecambe Bay and the Kent estuary.

Route Directions (Arnside to Arnside Tower via Knott)
Arnside was originally a tiny, remote fishing village which later
developed into a small port serving Kendal and Milnthorpe. Up to
1854 it even had its own Customs House but the coming of the railway
and the silting up of the Kent estuary killed the river traffic and brought
Arnside's role as a minor port to an end. In the long run the construc-

tion of the Furness Railway proved to be a blessing, it broke down the isolation of the area for the first time and gave Arnside a new lease of life as a quiet, 'select' holiday resort. Nowadays its popularity and accessibility have increased as a result of the M6 motorway.

It is the railway era that has left the greatest impression on the appearance of Arnside; the embankment and viaduct across the estuary was built in 1857 and rests on fifty piers.

Start by walking along the promenade and taking the shore path (public footpath sign to New Barns Bay). By a coastguard notice and two benches, turn left up a steep enclosed path and on reaching the road, turn right.

Turn left at the narrow lane which ascends Arnside Knott and just before the parking area, by a view indicator board, bear left and climb up the stony path to the summit. The view from here, across the Kent estuary and Morecambe Bay to the Cumbrian mountains beyond, can hardly be surpassed by any in the Lake District and affords an excellent excuse for a rest.

From the summit keep in the same direction, taking the obvious path ahead through the trees, across an open grassy area and into woodland again, bearing right and plunging steeply downhill (by a wall on the left) to a road. Turn right, and with a good view of Arnside Tower ahead, walk along the road to a farm track where you turn left, past the farm and on to the tower.

Arnside Tower
During the three centuries following Edward I's attempted conquest

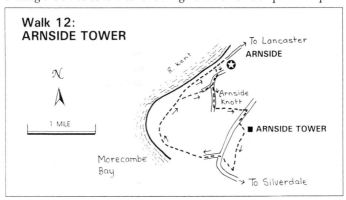

of Scotland and the English defeat by Robert Bruce at Bannockburn in 1314, there were many Anglo-Scottish wars and an ever present threat both of invasions by Scottish armies and raids by individual Scottish marauders. As a result many of the contemporary manor houses in the north of England were built in the form of fortified towers called 'pele towers'. These were especially numerous in Northumberland and Cumbria, though some are found in Lancashire as well, one of the most southerly being at Turton.

Arnside Tower was one of a chain of pele towers built around Morecambe Bay to protect the area from possible coastal incursions. Little is known about it except that it dates from sometime around the middle of the 14th century. Part of it blew down in a great gale in 1602 and subsequent centuries of neglect and Cumbrian weather have taken their toll, but it is still an impressive looking structure.

Route Directions (Arnside Tower to Arnside via Coast)
With your back to the tower, go through the metal gate (ignoring the ladder-stile on your left) and follow the broad clear track, with woods on the left, through another gate, soon joining a tarmac road through a caravan site. Just before reaching the end of a belt of trees, turn right along a rather indistinct path to a gate in the fence ahead. Over to the left are fine views of Morecambe Bay. Head across the field in front, over a gap in the wall, and up to the road. Cross over and walk down the lane opposite, past a group of cottages and through a caravan site, following public footpath signs to White Creek.

You now join the coast and the next 1.5 miles are particularly attractive. The route is along a clear and easy, wooded path that follows the line of low cliffs, at first by the edge of Morecambe Bay and then bearing right along the south side of the Kent estuary. When the tide is out you can walk along the sea marshes below the cliffs instead, for the first half-mile or so. There are plenty of rocks that make good picnic places and the combination of sea, river, cliffs and woodland is extremely pleasant. Keep following the signs to Arnside all the time and, soon after passing through another small caravan site, the path veers slightly to the right away from the estuary to cross a small creek. In front you get your first view of the railway viaduct at Arnside.

At this point you have the choice of two alternative routes back to Arnside. You can either keep to the right along a straight farm track or turn left and follow the shore.

URBAN AND MARITIME HERITAGE

The long coastline of north-west England, stretching from the Solway Firth facing Scotland to the Dee estuary overlooking Wales, has always had a great military and commercial significance. Coastal defences range from Roman forts, the medieval (and subsequent modernised) castles of Lancaster and Chester, to the remains of Merseyside's Second World War anti-aircraft defences.

The following group of walks concentrate more on a commercial theme, focusing on two river estuaries and their ports, both of which were engaged in a long, and ultimately unsuccessful, battle to maintain their status and prosperity against a constantly rising tide of silt and mud that resulted in the virtual 'choking-up' of these estuaries.

From Roman times to the 15th century Chester was England's major west coast port, and the River Dee an important commercial and military waterway. When the river began to silt up attempts to prolong its trade by developing new ports downstream at Neston and Parkgate failed, and Chester and the Dee were superseded by Liverpool and the Mersey.

Similarly Lancaster and the River Lune rose to a position of commercial greatness in the 18th century, largely through the extensive transatlantic trade with America and the West Indies, but declined for the same reason. Here again efforts were made to keep the Lune trade going by establishing ports further down the river, first at Sunderland and later at Glasson Dock, but these only enjoyed a brief period of importance and lost out to more favourably situated ports such as Preston, Heysham and Barrow.

In the process of pursuing this theme of maritime decline, you not only see some attractive coastal scenery, but also follow a disused railway line (now Country Park) and explore the two most historic and fascinating cities of the north-west.

Christmas Festivities in the medieval streets of Chester

13. CHESTER

Start and Finish: The Cross, in front of St. Peter's Church
Distance: 2.5 miles   *Approximate Time:*   2 hours
Parking: Chester
Refreshments: An almost bewildering choice of eating and drinking places in Chester

General Description

Chester is one of the great showcases of Europe with a history going back to the foundation of the fort of Deva by the Romans in the 1st century A.D. There is such a wealth of historic attractions that this walk can serve as no more than an appetiser. It seeks to highlight both the variety and continuity of Chester's past as a maritime, commercial, administrative, military and ecclesiastical centre, and also its present status as a popular residential, shopping and tourist centre. By far the pleasantest and most convenient way to appreciate this enormous span of history is by strolling along the circuit of medieval walls. From many points on these walls the hills of North Wales are clearly visible on the horizon - a constant reminder of Chester's major role in the Middle Ages as a vital border stronghold, both guarding England from Welsh raids, and serving as a springboard and supply point for English incursions by land and sea into Wales and across to Ireland.

Route Directions (The Cross to the Castle)
The walk begins at The Cross, centre of Chester for nearly 2,000 years, where the four principal streets of Roman Deva met and where their successors have continued to do the same ever since. The Cross is in fact the medieval High Cross which was restored to its original position in front of St. Peter's Church in 1975, having been removed and broken up, probably during the Cromwellian era. St. Peter's stands on the site of the principia, the headquarters building of the Roman fort.

Glancing around, you are immediately aware of the feature that is unique to Chester - the Rows, a series of two-tiered covered walkways with shops at both street and first floor level, and continuous

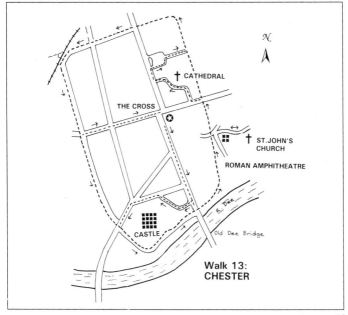

Walk 13:
CHESTER

balconies on the upper level from which you can look down on the street below. Why these are found only in Chester is a mystery which has never been satisfactorily explained despite numerous ingenious theories. All that can be said with certainty is that they are confined within the limits of the Roman fortress and are first referred to in 14th century records. Their black and white appearance looks authentically Tudor, but they are mostly Victorian restorations though none the less attractive for that.

Start by walking along Bridge Street, utilising the the Rows if you like, and continuing down Lower Bridge Street. On the way you pass, on the right, three particularly outstanding black and white 17th century buildings, now all inns - the Falcon, King's Head, and Bear and Billet respectively. Just before the Bear and Billet, turn right into Shipgate Street and right again up St. Mary's Hill. At the top turn left, by the side of the mainly 15th-16th century St. Mary's Church to enter a large, open space around which are grouped the buildings that make up Chester Castle.

Chester Castle

This is not a conventional castle, but an assortment of buildings from the 13th to the 20th centuries that reflect Chester's continuous importance as a military and administrative centre. These comprise the 13th century Agricola Tower (only remaining part of the large medieval fortress), an array of early 19th century buildings that include barracks, assize court, and Museum of the Cheshire Regiment, and also the Cheshire County Hall, begun in 1938 and completed in 1957.

The original Norman castle, strengthened by Henry III in the 13th century, was one of the key fortresses along the Welsh border. It was Edward I's principal base for the conquest of Wales and was also used as a launching pad for expeditions to Ireland. As guardian of the Welsh Marches, the powerful earls of Chester enjoyed the status and privileges of semi-independent princes. When the male line died out in 1237, the earldom reverted to the Crown and ever since Earl of Chester has been one of the titles held by the male heir to the throne, along with that of Prince of Wales.

Between 1789 and 1813 the medieval castle was largely pulled down and replaced by Thomas Harrison's imposing Classical structures. Particularly impressive is the Grand Entrance, which you make your way through on to Grosvenor Road.

Route Directions (Castle to the Roman Amphitheatre)

Turn left along Grosvenor Road and left again into Castle Drive. Here you join the walls near their south-western corner and the rest of the route is mostly along the top of the walls, apart from the final stretch and two short diversions to view places of interest. Follow the walls around by the castle buildings and along the road, past County Hall (from where there is a good view of the 14th century Old Dee Bridge, until 1831 the main route into North Wales), and on to Bridgegate. Although Chester retains its complete circuit of medieval walls, it has none of the original gateways - these were all rebuilt in later centuries to ease the flow of traffic. Bridgegate dates from 1782.

After keeping by the River Dee for a short while above a weir, the walls turn north, now raised high above street level. On the left is Park Street containing a row of fine 17th century half-timbered cottages. On the right is the Roman Garden, containing remains of Roman columns and an example of a hypocaust, by which the Romans provided a central heating system for their buildings. At the next gateway, Newgate (1938), descend from the walls and turn right in order to visit the most impressive remains of Roman Chester.

Roman Amphitheatre

Although only half excavated (the other half lies underneath a convent), Chester's amphitheatre is the largest yet discovered in Britain. It is elliptical in shape, measuring 314 x 286 feet, and was built of stone towards the end of the 1st century A.D., replacing an earlier and smaller wooden one. It probably ceased to be used around the middle of the 4th century.

This was Deva's sports stadium, built, as was customary in Roman towns, outside the walls. Here would be held a variety of military, gladiatorial and hunting contests, (often of a cruel nature), for the purposes both of entertainment and military training.

St. John's Church

Chester is unusual in having two cathedrals and the first of these, St. John's Church, lies on the far side of the amphitheatre. After 1066 Peter, the first Norman bishop of Mercia, acting in line with a government policy to have cathedrals located in the main town of every diocese, moved his seat from Lichfield to Chester. He chose St. John's and began rebuilding the Saxon church already on the site. It only enjoyed cathedral status for a brief period, barely twenty years later his successor moved the headquarters to Coventry, then it alternated between Coventry and Lichfield for the remainder of the Middle Ages. When a separate diocese of Chester was created in 1541, the more centrally situated abbey of St. Werburgh was chosen for its cathedral.

Although much smaller than it was originally, and with both the east end and west tower in ruins, the church still retains its cathedral-like proportions and atmosphere, especially in the majestic late 11th century nave, the main surviving part of Bishop Peter's short-lived cathedral.

Route Directions (Roman Amphitheatre to the Cathedral)
Now for the real cathedral. Rejoin the walls at the Newgate and continue northwards. The eastern and northern sections of the medieval walls (from here to St. Martin's Gate) follow the line of the original Roman walls - the medieval walls encompassing a larger area than their Roman predecessors - and some of the Roman work remains. Continue over Eastgate (built in 1769 on the site of earlier medieval and Roman gateways and surmounted by a clock tower, erected in 1897 to commemorate Queen Victoria's Diamond Jubilee), and a little further on you come to the cathedral on your left. Turn left off the walls, past the modern Bell Tower (built 1974) into St. Werburgh Street and up to the cathedral entrance.

Chester Cathedral
Although one of the smaller English cathedrals, Chester has a number of unusual and interesting features. The original church on the site was founded in the early 10th century as a shrine for St. Werburgh, a 7th century Mercian princess. In 1093 this was re-established as a large Benedictine abbey by Hugh Lupus, first earl of Chester and nephew of William the Conqueror. This survived until 1541 when, following Henry VIII's dissolution of the monasteries, it was chosen as the cathedral for the new diocese of Chester, thus escaping the usual fate of ex-abbey churches i.e. either being relegated to parish church status, or falling into ruin.

Of this Norman abbey little is left apart from an 11th century arch in the north transept. The present Gothic church, built of rich red sandstone, is the result of extensive rebuilding throughout the 13th, 14th and 15th centuries. Externally the finest view is of the central tower and east end, as approached from the city walls; the west front is less impressive, being partially obscured by other buildings. Inside the cathedral you are aware of the disparity between the size of the transepts. The north one is very short, hemmed in by the adjoining monastic buildings, while the south one is much larger and more ornate, even wider than the main body of the cathedral. This is because the south transept once formed part of a parish church which was added to the cathedral in the 14th century.

Pride of Chester Cathedral are the magnificent and intricately-carved choir stalls dating from 1380 - an example of medieval crafts-manship at its very best. The 13th century lady chapel at the east end contains the remains of the shrine of St. Werburgh, a major centre of pilgrimage in the Middle Ages.

Because of its long monastic backgroud the attendant buildings on the north side of the cathedral are probably its most distinctive feature. The cloisters are complete and, leading off from them, is the superb monk's refectory with a wall pulpit from which one of the monks read to his colleagues during meals, and the fine 13th century chapter house approached via a vestibule that possesses some most exquisite stone vaulting.

Route Directions (Cathedral to The Cross)

Leaving the cathedral on the south side, continue up St. Werburgh Street and turn right into Northgate Street. Opposite is the ornate Victorian town hall, opened in 1869. Turn right almost immediately through the 14th century Abbey Gateway into the quiet precincts of Abbey Square, lined with dignified 18th century houses. Cross the square and continue down Abbey Street to rejoin the walls, where you turn left.

You soon come to the prominent landmark of King Charles Tower, so called because Charles I is supposed to have watched the defeat of his forces at the battle of Rowton Moor from here in 1645. At this point the walls turn westwards and are joined by a canal below. Continuing over Northgate (1808) and St. Martin's Gate (1966) and past the Goblin Tower, you get fine views of the Welsh hills ahead before reaching the north-west corner of the walls at Bonewaldest-horne's Tower. In front a short spur of the walls leads to the 14th century Water Tower, which was once lapped by the waters of the River Dee and built to guard the port of Chester.

The Dee has changed course since the Middle Ages, up to the 15th century this western stretch of the wall overlooked what would have been a bustling harbour. A short distance from here is the Roodee, a large open space now partly used as a racecourse, which still contains remnants of quays built by the Romans. The port of Chester was at the height of its prosperity between the 12th and 14th centuries when there was considerable trade with Ireland, France, Spain, Portugal, the Baltic and Low Countries in commodities that included fish, wool, linen, wine, ironware, fruits, spices, cheese, salt and grain. At that time Chester was one of England's major ports and, as a consequence, the mayor of Chester was granted the title 'Admiral of the Dee', a title which, though largely meaningless, is still held today. It was during the 15th century that the river started to silt up and Chester's decline began. Attempts to maintain its trade, by establishing new ports further downstream at Neston and Parkgate, failed to overcome the silting problem and Chester and the Dee continued to decline, to be superseded by the hitherto unimportant Liverpool and the Mersey.

At Bonewaldesthorne's Tower follow the walls as they turn sharply to the south as far as the Watergate (rebuilt 1788). Here you leave the walls for the last time and turn left along Watergate Street to make your way back to The Cross. Watergate Street was the principal route from the harbour to the city centre and contains many fine buildings as evidence of former commercial prosperity. Look out in particular for Stanley Palace on the corner of the ring road, a superb black and white late 16th century town house, and a little further on where the Rows re-appear, Bishop Lloyd's House, built in the early 17th century and possessing marvellous carved timberwork.

The abiding impression of this walk around Chester is of a city with a long history, reflected by a variety of buildings (Roman, medieval, Tudor, Stuart, Georgian, Victorian and modern), all mixed together in an apparently harmonious fashion. Despite this mixture and the numerous phases in the city's development (Roman fort, medieval port, administrative and military stronghold, cathedral city and modern tourist centre), Chester basically retains the atmosphere and pattern of a medieval city. Its varied buildings from the 1st to the 20th centuries are huddled within the protective circuit of walls, and are dominated still by those twin symbols of medieval power, the castle and cathedral.

Once flourishing port, Parkgate now looks out over marshland

14. WIRRAL WAY

Start: Wirral Country Park (Thurstaston Visitor Centre)
Finish: Parkgate
Distance: 5.5 miles *Approximate Time:* 3 hours
Ordnance Survey Landranger Maps: 108 and 117
Parking: Thurstaston Visitor Centre
Refreshments: Pubs, restaurants and cafes in Parkgate
General Description
Suburban expansion and proximity to Liverpool have still left plenty of surprisingly peaceful, open countryside in the Wirral. This easy and attractive walk follows, for the most part, a disused railway line, finishing at Parkgate, once an imporant port for Ireland but now left high and dry by the silting up of the Dee. All the way there are fine views across the Dee estuary to the hills of North Wales.

Wirral Country Park
The Wirral Country Park is unique in that it is the only one based on a former railway line and for the most part it hardly extends beyond the width of the track.

In1865 a single track line was built along the western side of the Wirral peninsula, originally between Hooton and Parkgate, later extended to West Kirby (in 1896). The new line provided a link with both

Chester and Liverpool and as well as being used for goods transport (agricultural produce, coal, and later the products of the nearby Cadbury factory), helped to stimulate the development of the Wirral as a desirable commuter area for Merseyside. The decline of rail traffic after the Second World War led to the line's inevitable closure; passenger traffic ceased in 1956 and the line finally closed to goods traffic in 1962.

Fortunately Cheshire County Council had the foresight to recommend that the disused line should become the focal point of a linear country park and be turned into a public footpath and bridleway. The result is a fascinating 12 mile route running through cuttings and above embankments along the whole length of the former line, except for two short breaks where the track was developed before the idea of the country park was decided upon.

At Thurstaston Visitor Centre, built on the site of one of the stations, there are displays illustrating the history of the railway and the surrounding area and its transformation into a country park, an

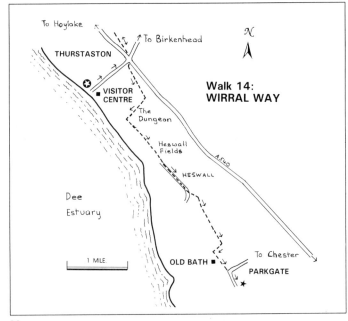

audio-visual programme and a variety of guidebooks and leaflets. Remains of the platforms can still be seen. On the adjoining grassy clifftop, there are fine views over the Dee estuary and the site of a Second World War anti-aircraft gun platform, part of Merseyside's wartime defences.

Route Directions

Turn right out of the Visitor Centre and walk along the road to Thurstaston village, about 0.5 mile. In the village turn right and immediately left up to the main road. Turn left and, soon after passing in front of the Cottage Loaf Restaurant, bear right over a stile and along the sandy track ahead between gorse bushes. In front of a school building turn left and climb to the summit of Thurstaston Hill (255 feet). Despite its modest size it is the highest point in the area and its sandstone outcrops provide a magnificent panoramic view that takes in the whole of the Wirral, the Dee estuary, the hills of North Wales, the Mersey estuary and the buildings in Liverpool city centre.

Descend and retrace your steps to Thurstaston village. Thurstaston still has something of the atmosphere of an old rural village with church and hall side by side. The red sandstone church, built in 1886, is the third on the site and in one corner of the churchyard the tower of the second church, dating from 1824, still stands. The adjoining hall is a mixture of periods and styles; the oldest parts go back to the 14th century.

The route continues along the lane to the left of the church. Where the lane bends to the left continue along a broad path which you follow in a straight line over three stiles. To the right the views over the Dee are superb and behind there is a particularly picturesque view of Thurstaston village, huddled around the church and hall with the church spire standing out prominently. After climbing the third stile you follow the narrow path ahead between a hedge and wire fence. Approaching a belt of trees there are two stiles; climb over the first but, before the second one, turn right on to a flagged path through an attractive wooded dell called the Dungeon.

Follow a stream downhill along the side of a virtual gorge which is quite steep in places. There are paths both sides of the stream and it does not matter which side you take. Eventually you pick up a path on the left-hand side of the stream that follows the edge of the trees (wire fence on the left) and continues downhill, out of the trees and into more open country. When you reach some steps, climb them and turn left. You are now on the Wirral Way and the rest of the route is mostly along the straight, flat, easy to follow disused railway track.

The path is very pleasant and gaps in the hedges on both sides reveal fine views over fields and wooded hills to the left and meadows, marsh, estuary and the Welsh hills to the right. Continue past modern residential property on the edge of Heswall and where there is a temporary break in the former railway track, keep on along the road (Davenport Road) regaining the Wirral Way after just over 0.25 mile, at a Wirral Country Park signpost. Walk along the straight track again as far as Backwood Hall Bridge, where you turn left up the steps and left over the bridge heading towards the estuary. At the foreshore turn left along a path, past the walls of Parkgate Old Bath (now a car park) and continue on the road into Parkgate.

Parkgate

There are no outstanding individual buildings in Parkgate, it is the overall impression that counts. Parkgate is a delightful village of whitewashed cottages and half-timbered buildings, with the air of a place that has been passed-by.

In the Middle Ages the Dee was a far more important commercial waterway than the Mersey, and Chester was a leading port when Liverpool was comparatively insignificant. However since the late 14th century the Dee has been slowly silting up, and this led to the decline and eventual abandonment of Chester as a port, and to the development of alternative ports downstream - first Neston and, in the 18th century, Parkgate.

Parkgate was at its height in the 18th century when it was a busy, bustling port with ferries plying across the river to Flint and a flourishing passenger trade with Ireland. At that time it possessed a theatre, assembly rooms, customs house, inns, gambling parlours and coffee houses - difficult to imagine when strolling around this quiet backwater today. Handel is supposed to have added the final touches to the 'Messiah' when staying here in 1746 while waiting to catch a boat to Dublin.

The silting up of the river continued relentlessly and doomed Parkgate as a port, as it had earlier done for Chester and Neston. Attempts were made to promote the village as a fishing port and in the 19th century it became for a while a holiday resort. The Parade, lined with 17th-19th century buildings, still retains something of the atmosphere of a fashionable promenade. Parkgate Old Baths, passed towards the end of the walk, were built in 1923 as a holiday attraction and were filled with sea water at high tide. Even that role disappeared in the 1930's; the baths closed in 1942 and now the water is a mile away across the thick marshes, leaving Parkgate as a monument to what might have been but for the vagaries of the river - a second Liverpool perhaps.

To return to your starting point you have two alternatives:

1.　　Catch a bus (C22) from Parkgate to Heswall, another (183) from Heswall to Thurstaston (for details phone 051 342 6101) and then walk back along the road to the Visitor Centre.

2.　　If you are feeling refreshed after a meal and a drink in Parkgate, and you have the time, walk back along the Wirral Way.

Georgian elegance - The Old Town Hall at Lancaster

15. LANCASTER

Start and Finish: Gatehouse of Lancaster Castle
Distance: 2 miles   *Approximate Time:* 1hr 30 mins
Parking: Lancaster
Refreshments: Plenty of choice in Lancaster
General Description
The view from Castle Hill clearly reveals Lancaster's strategic significance as one of the key defensive strongholds in the country: lying above a river between the hills and the sea, commanding the main western route between England and Scotland and standing at the southern gateway to the Lake District, whose mountains can be seen across Morecambe Bay. The positioning of the castle and priory side by side on a steep hill overlooking the Lune is reminiscent of Durham. This walk fuses together the four main strands in Lancaster's long history: Roman, medieval, Georgian and Victorian.

Lancaster Castle
Here are no mellowed, ivy-covered ruins but grim and powerful walls, rebuilt and strengthened many times to enable Lancaster Castle to retain at least two of its original roles - law court and prison. Few places in England, other than the Tower of London, can match its macabre atmosphere, not surprising in a place associated so much with human cruelties and sufferings. Many prisoners have suffered incarceration, torture and execution within its walls. Amongst the notorious trials held here were that of John Paslew (last abbot of Whalley) in 1536, the Pendle witches in 1612, numerous Catholic priests in the late 16th and early 17th centuries, Jacobite rebels after the 1715 and 1745 uprisings and, in more recent years the Birmingham pub bombers in 1975 and the 'Handless Corpse' drugs trial in 1981.

The oldest part is the massive keep or Lungess Tower, 80 feet square and first built by Roger de Poitou around 1090. The curtain walls, towers and John of Gaunt's great gatehouse were constructed in the late 14th and early 15th centuries, rebuilt and extended in the late 18th century when the castle was enlarged to serve as the Assize Courts and County Jail. It was at this time that the spacious semi-circular Shire Hall was built.

Royal connections began with the marriage of Blanche, daughter of the duke of Lancaster, to John of Gaunt, fourth son of Edward III and one of the castle's most powerful figures. Their son overthrew Richard II in 1399 and became Henry IV, first of the Lancastrian kings. Since his time all monarchs, queens as well as kings, have held the title of Duke of Lancaster.

As a major royal fortress occupying such a strategic position, Lancaster was involved in most of the important national upheavals. It saw action in the Wars of the Roses and the 17th century Civil War between Charles I and Parliament, and was captured by Jacobite forces in both the 1715 and 1745 rebellions.

Lancaster Castle is still used as a prison, because of this visitors are taken on a restricted tour of the buildings, starting with the 18th century Shire Hall (with its vast array of shields) and including the Crown Court and dungeons. The original impression of grimness is further reinforced inside where you see various instruments of torture, the branding irons, the dark miserable cells and the notorious Drop Room where, as the name so chillingly suggests, prisoners were prepared for execution. From this room they passed through a door outside to 'Hanging Corner' where public executions were held until as late as 1865, watched sometimes by thousands of spectators.

Lancaster Priory
Beside the castle stands the mainly 15th century church, once part of a Benedictine priory. There was a Saxon church on the site (a doorway from this survives in the west wall of the nave), but the priory itself was

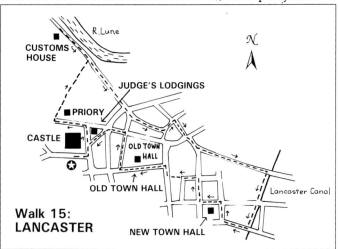

Walk 15:
LANCASTER

founded in 1094 by the same man, Roger de Poitou, who built the castle. It was one of a number of alien priories in England; this means that it was a dependency of a continental monastery, in Lancaster's case the abbey of Sees in Normandy. During the Hundred Years War with France, these alien priories were regarded with suspicion, almost as enemy territory, and in 1414 they were suppressed by Henry V.

Lancaster Priory was given to the Brigittine nuns of Syon in Middlesex who, in 1420, installed a vicar. Thus the priory became the parish church and was rebuilt in the 15th century in its present form. It certainly looks like a conventional large 'town church' of the period and there are no monastic remains - they lay to the south of the church in what is now a garden and field. The western tower was rebuilt in the 18th century.

Inside, the church is spacious and dignified but its great glory are the superb, elaborately-carved, late medieval choir stalls. It is thought that these might have come from either Cockersand or Furness after these monasteries were dissolved, but there is no definite evidence for this.

Route Directions (Castle to the Customs House)
All around the castle are fine examples of 18th century houses, symbols of Lancaster's growth and prosperity at that time, the reason for which will become apparent on reaching the river.

From the front of the church follow the public footpath (sign-posted to the Maritime Museum) downhill, with fields on both sides. The field on the left contains earthworks (part of both the Roman and medieval defences of Lancaster), as well as a panoramic view over the Lune estuary, Morecambe Bay and the Lakeland mountains. A short detour across the field on the right brings you to the fragmentary remains of a 4th century fort, the only piece of Roman Lancaster still visible on its original site.

Continue down the main path, over a footbridge and down some steps to the river. Turn left along St. George's Quay, past impressive 18th century warehouses, to the Maritime Museum, housed in the old Customs House.

Customs House (Maritime Museum)
During the late 17th and 18th centuries there was a great expansion in transatlantic trade between Britain and her American and Caribbean

colonies, and Lancaster became one of the important west coast ports handling this trade. St. George's Quay was built around the middle of the 18th century and it was over the next three decades that most of the handsome Georgian buildings were erected: the numerous town houses of the wealthy merchants, quayside warehouses and Old Town Hall. Possibly the most handsome of all is the beautifully proportioned Customs House, built in 1764 and designed by Richard Gillow of the well-known local furniture company. It is appropriate that this building is now used as the Maritime Museum, depicting the rise and fall of the port of Lancaster and surrounding Morecambe Bay area in a particularly fascinating and imaginative manner.

The town's prosperity as a port reached its height in the second half of the 18th century. Among the main commodities that passed through Lancaster were sugar, coffee, rum, cotton, timber and the lucrative trade in slaves. In the following century the port declined, partly because of the continual silting up of the Lune and partly because it was too far away from the main manufacturing centres further south. Efforts to counteract both problems, by developing ports downstream first at Sunderland and later at Glasson, and constructing the Lancaster Canal to provide a link to Preston, were of no avail and Lancaster continued to lose out to Liverpool, Preston, Fleetwood, Heysham and Barrow. Yet the Georgian streets and squares, St. George's Quay and especially the Customs House remain as testimony to this thriving epoch in Lancaster's history.

Route Directions (Customs House to the Castle)
Retrace your steps along St. George's Quay and continue as far as the main road, where you take a sharp turn to the right up China Street to the Judge's Lodgings. This large and elegant 17th century building, which pre-dates Lancaster's 18th century boom period, was originally a family home, later a residence of the judges during trials at the castle, and is now used as a dual museum of childhood and the Gillow furniture business.

Turn left along Church Street (more fine Georgian buildings), left into North Road and bear right to the 18th century St. John's Church. Turn right again and left along Moor Lane, past the Duke's Playhouse, to the canal bridge. At the bridge turn left down the steps and right at the bottom to pass under the bridge.

Now you come to Victorian Lancaster. The canal itself was built to link Lancaster with industrial Lancashire and there are some fine examples of 19th century mills by the canalside. As you walk along the towpath you get clear views on the left of two other buildings of that period: the Catholic cathedral (1857-59) with its spire and, on the skyline, the Ashton memorial (1909), built just a few years after the Victorian era by Lord Ashton, the local industrialist, as a memorial to his wife. Leaving the canal at the second bridge, turn right along the road, take the first turn on the right and then left to enter Dalton Square. Here is the largest of Lancaster's public buildings, the New Town Hall, financed by Lord Ashton and opened in 1909.

Passing in front of the Town Hall turn right, first left into Gage Street and continue ahead into the pedestrianised shopping area. Turn right and first left into the Market Square, dominated by the Old Town Hall (1781-83), now the Lancaster City Museum. Walk past the Old Town Hall for a few yards and turn right down Music Room Passage to see the small 18th century Music Room, possibly the most perfect of all Lancaster's Georgian buildings, originally thought to have been a pavilion or summer house for one of the large town houses.

Continue to the end of the passage, turn left along Church Street, over the main road and up the hill past the Judge's Lodgings back to the castle gatehouse.

The scanty remains of St. Patrick's Chapel at Heysham

16.   HEYSHAM AND SUNDERLAND POINT

Start: Heysham village (from Morecambe follows signposts to Lower Heysham)

Finish: Overton

Distance: 7 miles   *Approximate Time:* 3.5 hours

Ordnance Survey Landranger Maps: 97 and 102

Parking: Heysham

Refreshments: Pubs and cafes in Heysham, pubs in Overton

General Description

Buildings as diverse as Saxon churches, 18th century cotton warehouses, and the 20th century holiday camps and power station jostle for position on the narrow peninsula that lies between Morecambe Bay and the Lune estuary. Despite the proximity of industrial and large resorts, sections of this walk, especially across the bleak coastal marshes near Sunderland Point, have an air of remoteness hard to find in any other part of Lancashire.

Heysham

Heysham village is a quiet oasis of old cottages surrounded by the suburban sprawl of Morecambe, industrial estates and harbour. From the centre a short stroll along Main Street brings you to the headland that is the oldest Christian site in Lancashire and one of the earliest and most interesting in the country, associated with that misty and largely unknown period in our history between the departure of the Romans and the coming of the Normans when Celtic saints, Saxon conquerors and Viking marauders all left their mark on this area of the Lancashire coast. There are two adjacent churches; just below the headland the parish church of St. Peter, and above it the scanty ruins of St. Patrick's Chapel, both of which were built before the Norman Conquest.

The small attractive church, thought to be founded in the 10th century, is a rather confusing mixture of styles and ages but contains a lot of Norman work and retains some of the original Saxon church, notably the west wall. Of particular interest is the fine 12th century arch leading into the chancel and the rare and fascinating hogback stone. A hogback was a covering over a tomb of an important person and the intricate carvings of hunting and battle scenes suggest that it was Norse, possibly commemorating some 10th century Viking chief. It originally stood in the churchyard where over the centuries, it became covered with vegetation and was only discovered around 1800 when it was brought inside for protection.

The ruins of St. Patrick's Chapel are even more difficult to date and there is a legend that the chapel was founded by St. Patrick himself, when shipwrecked on the shore below while journeying between Ireland and Scotland. It is definitely older than the church but could be 8th or 9th century, of Celtic or Saxon origin. Although there is very little left, the tiny chapel (when complete it only measured 23 x 8 feet) commands an extensive view over Morecambe Bay with a sandy beach below, and the Lakeland mountains on the horizon. There is another hogback stone nearby but the most interesting features surrounding the chapel are the unique tombs cut into the sandstone rock: six main ones above the chapel and another two below it.

Heysham headland is a rare surviving example of an early Christian coastal settlement and the co-existence of a possibly Celtic chapel, Viking hogback stone and Saxon church on the one small site, together with the unusual rock tombs, gives it a unique interest.

Route Directions (Heysham to Sunderland Point)
From St. Patrick's Chapel make your way along the headland towards

Heysham harbour, which comes into view almost immediately. If the tide is out the best way is to walk along the beach as the cliff-top path is not very clear. If you do have to stick to the top, you come out on a road for about 100 yards but, where the road veers left, you take the rather indistinct path that continues straight ahead. On reaching the harbour turn left along the road.

The next part of the walk is frankly rather tedious as it involves 2 miles of unavoidable road walking past housing estates, industrial sites and caravan parks with Heysham power station on the right. It has to be viewed as part of the constantly changing pattern of the landscape in this part of Lancashire and there is some compensation in distant views of the Bowland Fells to the east and, in particular, the solitude and fascination of Sunderland Point to come.

After leaving the harbour keep on where the main road bears left and follow the minor road as it curves right and then left to go uphill. There is a paved footpath on the left-hand side. At a T-junction turn right and then keep right again when you shortly join the main A589.

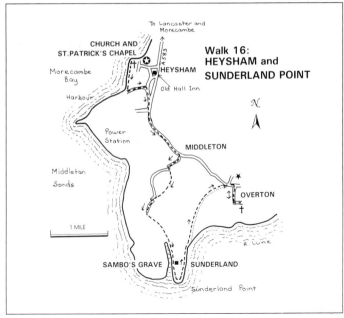

Keep along the road (path on the right-hand side for much of the way) for 1.25 miles, follow signs to Middleton and Overton.

Approaching Middleton the scenery starts to become more open and rural and in the village you turn right along Carr Lane following signs to Middleton Sands. Keep along the lane as it curves to the right, bends sharply to the left and then almost immediately right again. At this point you take to the fields by going through a gate ahead. If the weather has been wet and the fields are muddy, you may prefer to continue along the lane which is rejoined a little further on.

Follow the left-hand edge of the field, turn left through the first gate and then right along the right-hand edge of the next field, following the hedge round to the right to climb a ladder-stile. Then turn left along the edge of the field (hedge and wire fence on the left), climb the stile ahead and continue in the direction of some farm buildings. Keep on into the next field (wire fence on right), turn sharp right over a ladder-stile and head in a straight line for the farm buildings in front along the top of a raised embankment. Turn left when you rejoin the lane and follow it as it meanders between trees and cottages to end at a beach car park.

Here you turn left and follow the clear, broad track for 1.5 miles across the flat, lonely, desolate coastal marshes towards Sunderland Point. The houses and trees of the hamlet of Sunderland can be seen ahead and the track is easy to follow, keeping to the right-hand side of a wire fence for much of the way. Here is a complete contrast to the earlier, urbanised section of the walk: a feeling of genuine remoteness and isolation, though a glance behind will still reveal the 20th century presence of the power station. All around are extensive views: to the right over the sea, in front towards the point and the Fylde Coast on the other side of the estuary, and to the left, across the Lune, the buildings of Lancaster with the hills of the Forest of Bowland beyond. Take a look at Sambo's Grave where you see the notice, an indication that Sunderland Point is not far away. Sambo was a Negro slave who accompanied his master, a cotton merchant, to England. While on business in Lancaster master and slave became separated and the legend says that the loyal Sambo died of grief, or was it disease or perhaps something to do with the Lancashire climate? Whatever the reason the heathen slave could not be buried in consecrated ground, and therefore his grave lies in this utterly remote and windswept spot that could not be further removed from the warmer climes with which he would have been familiar.

After Sambo's Grave continue on to round the point itself and then keep along the north bank of the estuary into Sunderland Point.

Sunderland Point

It is hard to imagine that this tiny, remote, lonely hamlet was once a flourishing port. In the 18th century cargoes of cotton, rum, sugar and tobacco were landed here and it was the profits made from trade in these commodities, plus those from slavery, that created the fine Georgian buildings that grace the city of Lancaster. Indeed perhaps the Lancashire cotton industry itself had its origins here as it was alleged that the first consignment of raw cotton from the American colonies was landed on this spot.

The port of Sunderland was established in the early 18th century by Robert Lawson, a Quaker merchant from Lancaster who built the quays and warehouses down on the Lune estuary to try and overcome the problem of the river silting up. It enjoyed only a brief heyday, as the silting up continued, and towards the end of the 18th century it was largely superseded by Glasson Dock on the opposite bank. Its remoteness made it impossible to develop into either a resort, like Morecambe and Heysham, or a centre for pleasure boating like Glasson Dock.

Like all 'ghost towns' Sunderland has an attractive melancholic air. Two rows of 18th century warehouses, now mainly converted into houses, some cottages plus the quay are all that remain. Apart from Sambo's Grave there are two surviving links with the days of transatlantic trade. In front of the Cotton Tree Barn grows what is always referred to as the cotton tree, though it is in fact a kapok tree. Even more incongruous is the large detached house of Sunderland Hall which, with its verandas and canopies, resembles the residence of a plantation owner and would not look out of place in the Caribbean or American's Deep South. No wonder that sailors, looking forward to the more robust and down-to-earth pleasures of larger ports, nicknamed Sunderland Point 'Cape Famine'.

Route Directions (Sunderland Point to Overton)

The best route to Overton when the tide is out is to walk along the narrow lane across the marshes, a distance of about 1.5 miles. Overton is an attractive village with some 18th century fishermens' cottages and a tiny, picturesque Norman church, about 0.5 mile from the village centre in a superb position above the Lune directly opposite Glasson Dock. Like the church at Heysham it has some Saxon stonework on the west wall.

There is a regular bus service from Overton back to Heysham and details are available from Morecambe Tourist Information Office (0524 414110). Get off in Heysham at the Old Hall Inn, turn left and then immediately right along School Road. When you come to a T-junction, turn left and proceed downhill into the centre of Heysham village, a distance of no more than 0.5 mile.

N.B. The road from Sunderland to Overton is flooded for several hours at high tide and therefore it is most important that you check on the times of the tides before starting the walk. Morecambe Tourist Information Office will provide details (0524 414110).

Glasson Dock - eighteenth century port now enjoying a revival

17. GLASSON DOCK AND COCKERSAND ABBEY

Start and Finish: Glasson Dock
Distance: 6 miles   *Approximate Time:* 3 hours
Ordnance Survey Landranger Map: 102
Parking: Glasson Dock
Refreshments: Pubs and cafes at Glasson Dock

General Description
This is a fresh, easy-paced coastal walk that links an 18th century port on the lower reaches of the Lune with the ruins of a 13th century abbey. The first part is along the southern shore of the Lune estuary, the latter part along the towpath of the Lancaster Canal and all the way there are extensive views across the Fylde towards the Bowland Fells.

Glasson Dock
Glasson Dock recalls the 18th century heyday of Lancaster as a port

when its extensive transatlantic trade in slaves, rum, tobacco, sugar and cotton brought great prosperity, as reflected in the fine Georgian buildings of the city. It came into existence, in fact, in an attempt to safeguard this prosperity. The trouble was that Lancaster's commercial life was threatened by the silting up of the Lune and, to offset this, new ports were developed lower down the river, first at Sunderland Point on the north side of the estuary (this was unsuccessful), and in 1787 at Glasson on the south side.

Almost from the start Glasson Dock was a white elephant despite strenuous efforts to make it a going concern. The problem was not simply the silting up of the Lune. Lancaster was too remote from the main centres of population and industry in south Lancashire, and there was too much competition from other north-west ports such as Preston and Heysham. The Lancaster Canal was constructed in 1797 to solve the problem of communication with the urban areas further south, and a branch to Glasson Dock was opened in 1826. Later, in 1883, a railway was built linking Glasson Dock with the main line at Lancaster, the former track of which now serves as the Lune Estuary Footpath. It was all to no avail. Glasson Dock never prospered and commercial traffic on the Lune continued to decline. Today, however, it enjoys a welcome revival as a small port and a centre for pleasure boating, the canal basin forming an attractive marina.

Route Directions (Glasson Dock to Cockersand Abbey)
From the car park cross the bridge over the canal basin opposite the Victoria Hotel, and walk up Tithe Barn Hill, the only bit of uphill

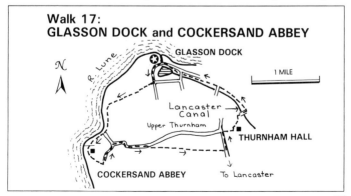

walking on the entire route. Bear left at the top and, where the road bends sharply to the left, turn right along a metalled lane which later becomes a farm track. Follow it through two gates down to a farm and, at the side of the farm, go through a gate and turn left to follow the tarmac track along the side of the Lune estuary. There are fine views across the estuary to the right and over the Fylde coastal marshes to the left, with the Bowland Fells on the skyline. Where the main track bears left keep straight on by the shore, and soon afterwards climb a stile and walk along the sea wall to the ruins of Cockersand Abbey.

Cockersand Abbey

The abbey stands in a lonely and remote spot overlooking the sea and coastal marshes and its ruins look even more forlorn than most. It was founded by William of Thurnham in 1184 and was inhabited by monks of the Premonstratensian Order. Its lands frequently suffered from flooding and the monks were responsible for reclaiming much of the surrounding area from the sea. Like all other monasteries it was closed down by Henry VIII in the 1530's.

Apart from a few crumbling walls the only part left is the 13th century octagonal chapter house. This was preserved because it was used by the Daltons of nearby Thurnham Hall as a family mausoleum.

Route Directions (Cockersand Abbey to Glasson Dock)

Follow the track past the abbey to the wall ahead, climb the steps, continue past the farm, through a gate and along the farm track to the road. Keep on along the road and follow it around several right angle turns. At a Y-fork bear right and, just past a cottage on the left where the road veers to the left, bear right across a footbridge. Walk along the edge of fields (there is a wire fence, or hedge and drainage channel on the right for most of the way) for about 1.25 miles, crossing several fences and stiles until you reach a farm. Keeping to the left of the farm buildings go through a white gate on to the road.

Turn left and follow the road for a short distance into the village of Upper Thurnham. At a public footpath sign to Galgate, turn right along the drive to Thurnham Hall.

Originally a 13th century pele tower, the present house was built in the 16th century, refronted in the 1820's and recently restored after becoming almost derelict. The castle-like appearance of the front of the house, which you see from the drive, is rather surprising for a domestic building of the 16th century. Its owners were the Daltons who, like many other Lancashire landowners, remained staunchly loyal to the Catholic faith during the Reformation. One member of the family, John Dalton, was imprisoned and fined for supporting the Catholic Old Pretender in the 1715 Jacobite Rebellion against George I. The hall is privately owned and not open to the public.

It is a pleasant and relaxing stroll of 1.5 miles from Thurnham Hall to Glasson Dock, mostly along the attractive towpath of the Lancaster Canal. Walk along the front of the hall, continue ahead over two stiles and bear slightly right towards a stone building in front. Go through a gate and bear right down to the canal bridge. Ahead is a lovely view of the Bowland Fells. Cross the bridge and turn left to join the towpath of the Glasson branch of the Lancaster Canal. Follow the right bank of the canal back to Glasson Dock, passing the small parish church on the right as you approach the canal basin.

HERITAGE OF GREAT HOUSES AND PARKS

In general the country houses of the north-west are more modest and less grandiose than their counterparts further south. The explanation for this lies in physical factors. The combination of damp climate and poor soil meant that there was not the wealth to sustain houses of great size and opulence. Proximity to the Scottish border and the unsettled nature of the region also meant that houses of a defensive nature, with battlemented towers and fortified gatehouses, were still being constructed in this part of the country long after these had been abandoned in favour of greater comfort and luxury elsewhere. A house of the same age as Hoghton Tower, built in, say, Warwickshire or Hampshire instead of Lancashire, would have a totally different appearance.

Exceptions can be found in the lusher, more fertile lowland areas of Cheshire, West Lancashire and the Vale of York that surround the hills, moors and mountains. Here there are great houses like Tatton, Lyme and Harewood, which can (surrounded by extensive landscaped parkland), rank among the finest in the country.

In the following selection of walks you get the opportunity to visit a wide cross-section of houses, ranging from what are basically modernised and enlarged medieval manor houses or pele towers, still with a military appearance, to some of the grand and elegant houses of the 17th, 18th and 19th centuries already mentioned. Their gardens and parklands often provide attractive, interesting and varied walking. In some cases the home and estate is still lived-in and owned by the same family who have occupied it since medieval times; in others it is maintained by the National Trust for our enlightenment and enjoyment. In two examples the house has totally disappeared but the surrounding park is preserved, one of these, in contrast to the conventional estates of the traditional landowning aristrocracy, was the creation of a philanthropic, self-made Victorian industrialist.

Deer still roam through Tatton Park

18. TATTON PARK

Start and Finish: Knutsford
Distance: 4.5 miles   *Approximate Time:* 2hrs 30 mins
Ordnance Survey Landranger Maps: 109 and 118
Parking: Knutsford
Refreshments: Pubs, cafes and restaurants in Knutsford, restaurant at Tatton Hall

General Description
From the attractive old town of Knutsford situated at the southern end of Tatton Park, this short and easy walk through woods, by meres and over the open grassland of the landscaped park of the Egerton family, illustrates the various changes throughout the ages in the life of a great country estate.

Tatton Hall and Park
Doing this circular walk in the recommended anti-clockwise direction is the best way of appreciating the evolution of the estate over the centuries. The first port of call is Tatton Old Hall, an excellent place to begin as the audio-visual programme in the former stables provides a

101

good introduction to the history of Tatton. The Old Hall is a 15th-16th century brick building which, after being abandoned, fell into ruin. Recently it has been restored and, inside, three rooms illustrate different periods in Tatton's history: the medieval Great Hall, the 17th century bedroom and the 19th century gamekeeper's cottage. The nearby village trail explains the activities and way of life of the medieval inhabitants of the village, (deserted and removed when the park was landscaped), by a series of information boards; an imaginative way of reconstructing the past in the absence of anything visual, apart from a few bumps in the ground!

In 1598 the Egertons became the owners of Tatton and the present hall, a grand and imposing classical mansion, was built for them on the site of an earlier house by Samuel and Lewis Wyatt between 1790 and 1815. From the fine entrance hall visitors tour the drawing room, music room, library and dining room etc., but the most unusual room is the Tenant's Hall, built by the last Lord Egerton to house his hunting trophies and now containing some of his old cars and various curiosities he collected. He was a remarkable and eccentric man, a great traveller, adventurer, hunter and an early pioneer of both motoring and aviation. Around the hall are colourful formal gardens which include a terraced Italian garden and a Japanese water garden.

The surrounding park was landscaped at about the same time as the hall was built, by Humphrey Repton, one of the most renowned

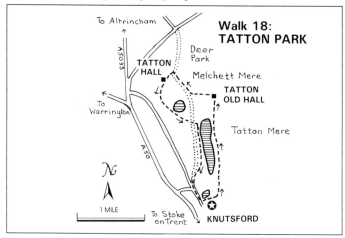

landscape architects of his day. He used the familiar combination of open grassland, random groups of trees and water to give the park a suitably 'natural' look. Tatton Mere was created by him but the smaller Melchett Mere only appeared in the 1920's, the result of subsidence from nearby salt mining.

Thus as we walk around we can see how Tatton has developed from a farming community huddled around the Old Hall to a landscaped park dominated by the present house, a familiar enough story in history of large English estates. The final stage in the evolutionary chain is also familiar; since 1958 Tatton Park has been owned by the National Trust and maintained by Cheshire County Council as an historic attraction and recreational amenity for the general public.

Route Directions

From the car park in Knutsford take the path across the recreation ground by the side of the mere. Soon after entering woodland, turn left through a gate to enter Tatton Park and follow the path through the woods. It is a most attractive path, first through thick woodland and later by the edge of Tatton Mere on the left, and after about a mile emerging into open grassland. Go through a gate near the end of the mere and bear half-right through a clump of trees to the Old Hall (clearly signposted).

From there it is a short and easy stroll, following the main drive, up to its grander and newer successor, clearly visible just over 0.5 a mile away.

After visiting the hall and garden leave by the main drive, follow the garden boundary around to the right and turn left along the beech avenue as far as the ice house. This is a mound in which ice was put and food stored to keep it cool; a method of keeping food fresh in pre-refrigeration days. Now you bear left across open grassland (no clear paths), skirting the edge of Melchett Mere, back to the main drive. Cross over and take the path that follows the other bank of Tatton Mere for a very pleasant walk to the main Knutsford entrance to the park, where you continue on into the main street.

Turton Tower - medieval pele tower subsequently enlarged

19. TURTON TOWER AND STONE CIRCLES

Start and Finish: Turton Tower
Distance: 4 miles   *Approximate Time:* 2hrs 30 mins
Ordnance Survey Landranger Map: 109
Parking: Small parking area near entrance to the tower
Refreshments: None
General Description
Though short and easy to follow the route involves some rough moorland walking. The focal point is a 15th century fortified house, built at a time of frequent Scottish raids. All the way there are extensive views over the surrounding moors and, at the highest point, you pass by the scanty remains of some prehistoric stone circles.

Route Directions (Turton Tower to the Stone Circles)
Follow the broad track past the entrance to the tower, passing on the right a water-wheel which came from a nearby mill and was installed here by the local Historical Society in 1978. Go over the elaborate battlemented 19th century railway bridge, built to harmonise with the

medieval structure of the tower, and continue through attractive woodland. At the junction of paths bear slightly right, go through a gate, and follow the broad track ahead as it winds its way gently uphill, over fields and by farms, giving grand views in all directions.

After just over a mile you reach a road where you keep straight on for about 100 yards and, at the end of a small plantation on the left, turn left over a stile and follow the fence on the left. Where the fence makes a left turn, bear half-right and head uphill across rough moorland. At this point there is no path to follow but the electricity pylon ahead acts as a useful guide. Go past the pylon, continue climbing more steeply and, at the top of the ridge, you get a splendid view over bare and bleak moorland with Rivington Moor and the Winter Hill television transmitter on the horizon. The television transmitter replaces the pylon as a convenient landmark and you start to descend, keeping in line with it, until you come to an embankment by a small stream where you pick up a recognisable path again. Follow it down, keeping the stream on your left and then veer right away from the stream, following the path downhill towards a clump of trees.

At the bottom of the hill turn left through a gate and follow a clear path ahead across the field to a stile. In front the view changes as you can see the buildings of Bolton and the built-up area of Greater Manchester beyond. Cross the stream and follow a very pleasant path ahead through gates, over stiles and past a barn for 0.75 mile, keeping roughly parallel with the ridge on your left. At the point where you enter a kind of funnel between converging walls, climb a stile and squeeze through the gap in the wall ahead. Head towards the farm in front but, after a few yards, turn left on to a narrow but clear path

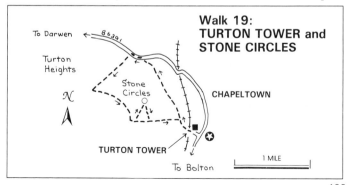

making towards the wall on your left. Keep parallel to the wall and where you join the path coming up from the farm on your right, turn left through a gap in the wall. At this point you can make a slight detour to see the stone circles by turning half-left and heading straight across the rough pasture, climbing steeply. There is no path but at the top the triangulation pillar, 1,075 feet high, acts as a landmark. The remains of the stone circles are close to it.

The Stone Circles

If you enjoy a short climb and like panoramic views the detour is well worthwhile, but if you are looking for something like a miniature version of Stonehenge you are in for a disappointment. There is little to see except for a few small and apparently random stones, but they do form part of a circle. When there were rather more left, 19th century antiquarians discovered a main circle with other small clusters of stones.

The site has never been investigated and nothing is known about it. All we can say is that it belongs to the prehistoric period and probably had some religious significance for the people who lived in the area at the time.

Route Directions (The Stone Circles to Turton Tower)

To get back on to the route to Turton stand with your back to the trig. point looking across to Winter Hill, turn left and follow the straight path across the moor downhill to rejoin the main path at the corner of a fence and wall. Climb a gate on the left and follow the path ahead keeping parallel with the wall on the right. Ahead are fine views over Holcombe Moor with Chapeltown in the valley below.

Walk on through a gap in the wall, go through the middle of a small wood and, keeping in line with the church tower ahead, make for a stile. Climb over and continue to the broad track where you turn right and retrace your steps to Turton Tower.

Turton Tower

Turton Tower is an irregular picturesque structure comprising a late medieval tower with Elizabethan and Victorian additions, standing in pleasantly secluded grounds. Originally it was a pele tower, built during the 15th century as a defence against Scottish raids by the Orrell family, who inherited the manor of Turton through marriage in 1420.

Like many Lancashire families the Orrells remained loyal to the Catholic faith at the time of the Reformation.

In the late 16th century William Orrell added the timber-framed entrance wing, but his extension led to financial difficulties and in 1628 the house was sold to Humphrey Cheetham, a wealthy and successful Manchester businessman who founded the school and hospital in the city that bears his name. After passing through several hands the house came into the possession of James Kay in 1835, another successful local businessman. He thoroughly restored it, rebuilding the east wing around what had been a Tudor farmhouse and adding the distinctive Dutch gables. His son helped to finance the construction of the Blackburn to Bolton railway, and it was he who built the nearby battlemented railway bridge. Turton Tower was sold again in 1890, and in 1930 was eventually given to the Turton Urban District Council who used part of it as a Council chamber. Nowadays it is maintained as a museum by Lancashire County Council.

The present appearance of the tower, both externally and internally, is mainly the work of James Kay. He panelled many of the rooms, though some of the panelling dates back to the 17th century, having been brought to Turton from other houses. There is plenty of fine, massive antique furniture to see, much of which came from the nearby demolished Bradshaw Hall, and in one of the upstairs rooms there is an exhibition depicting the history of the house and part of the library, originally bequeathed by Humphrey Cheetham to Turton church.

Turton Tower is an interesting example of a basically simple, medieval defensive structure which would originally have been rather cramped and dark, but which has been adapted and remodelled over succeeding centuries into a pleasant, light and comfortable home.

Fortified gatehouse of Hoghton Tower

20. WITTON COUNTRY PARK AND HOGHTON TOWER

Start: Witton Country Park - just off the A674 on the edge of Blackburn
Finish: Hoghton Tower
Distance: 4.5 miles *Approximate Time:* 2hrs 30 mins
Ordnance Survey Landranger Map: 103
Parking: Witton Country Park
Refreshments: Pubs in Hoghton
General Description
Starting in the attractive surroundings of Witton Country Park on the
western edge of Blackburn, this walk takes you across the hilly and
well-wooded country that lies between Blackburn and Preston, ending
at a 16th century fortified mansion in a commanding hilltop position.
Considering the proximity of main roads, railways and busy industrial
towns, the route is surprisingly rural and open.

Witton Country Park
Witton Country Park, it is hard to believe that the town centre of
Blackburn lies little more than a mile away. The area was once part of
the estates of the Feilden family, lords of the manor of Blackburn. After
being requisitioned by the army during the Second World War the
house and grounds were purchased by Blackburn Council for £64,000

in 1946, as a recreation area for the people of the town. The cost of repairing the badly neglected Witton House was too much, however, and it was demolished in the early 1950's. All that is left of the house, which was built around 1800, is the site and the stable-block.

The Country Park was created in 1973 and covers 472 acres. It comprises a mixture of woodland and grassland, retains some of the ornamental gardens of the Feildens and is noted for its extensive sports facilities.The stable-block now houses the Visitors Centre, a natural history exhibition, some horse-drawn carts and old farming implements.

Route Directions

From a former country estate where both the house and the family that occupied it have gone, we make our way to one where the house stands intact and is still lived-in by the descendants of the man who built it in the 16th century; an interesting comparison of the varying fortunes of landed estates and stately homes.

From the entrance to the Visitors Centre take the uphill path on the left, through rhododendron bushes to the plateau where a few stones mark the site of Witton House. Keeping to the left, go down some steps, along a woodland path, down more steps and, at the bottom, turn right and follow the path along the edge of the field. Cross a small stream and, bearing right by a wall, climb a stile and continue along the path through the woods with a wall on the left. There are some magnificent specimens of ancient trees on this section of the walk as you continue

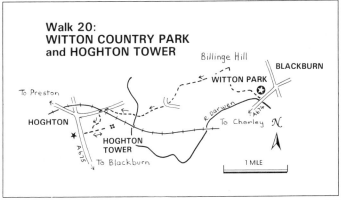

Walk 20:
WITTON COUNTRY PARK
and HOGHTON TOWER

along the clearly defined path, over another stream, up some steps and, bearing to the left, ahead over two pairs of stiles. The buildings of Blackburn can be seen over to the right and in front the thickly-wooded slopes of Billinge Hill (over 800 feet high). Continue uphill, over a stile by a farm, and then turn left along a farm track, at this point leaving the Country Park.

For most of the way there are fine views over to the left across the Darwen valley towards Pleasington, while on the right gorse bushes, silver birch and rough grassland make an almost primeval contribution to an otherwise gentle, pastoral landscape. Where the track bears slightly left towards a farm, keep straight ahead along a grassy path under an avenue of trees. Climb a stile by a house on the left and continue, keeping parallel with a wall on the left. In front you get a fine view of your objective - the abrupt wooded hill (over 500 feet high) on which Hoghton Tower stands.

Keeping by the wall on your left, follow it around to the right, through a gate and along a wide track. Where the track curves to the right, keep on past a farm to rejoin a wall on your left. At a junction of tracks bear left (still keeping by the wall) and, just before a stile ahead, turn right across a small area of rough ground down to a stile in a wire fence. Climb over and walk across the field ahead, keeping by a wire fence on the right. All around are views over pleasant rolling country. Soon the path becomes a broad farm track which you follow through a gate into the farmyard where you turn sharp left through another gate and, bearing half-right, head diagonally across the field towards a small bridge over a field drain. Keeping by the wire fence on the right, climb a fence, carry on through a gap in the fence in front and follow the path veering slightly to the left downhill. To the left Pleasington Priory and golf course are clearly visible. Make for a small gap in the trees ahead and continue downhill to a gate which brings you out on to a lane.

Turn right, and where the lane bends sharply to the right, keep on along a track (public footpath sign to Hoghton Bottoms) in front of a row of cottages. Follow the track as it winds downhill and, at a junction of tracks, keep left, go through a gate and follow another clear track downhill to a bridge over the River Darwen. Cross the river and continue to a lane. Cross straight over, climb a stile in the wall opposite and take the uphill path, over another stile, continuing uphill by a wall on the right. At the top go through a gate on to the road, turn left over the railway bridge (view of the walls of Hoghton Tower in front) and, near the first farm gate, turn left over a stile. Cross the field heading towards the woods in front, and at the wall turn right to follow the edge of the field across several stiles to the main drive to Hoghton Tower. Turn left to the entrance to the house.

Hoghton Tower

Despite being an Elizabethan building, Hoghton Tower has a severely medieval appearance, far removed from its more elegant and domesticated contemporaries further south; an indication of the still-troubled and lawless state of the north at the time. Its hilltop position adds to the fortress-like atmosphere.

Although the de Hoghton family have owned lands in the area since at least the 13th century, the present house was begun by Sir Thomas Hoghton in 1565. Like many other Lancashire landowners he remained true to the Catholic faith during the Reformation and died, in exile, in the Netherlands. Later de Hoghtons, however, accepted the reformed Protestant church, against Parliament in the Civil War and supported the Hanoverians during and fought both the Jacobite rebellions, thus escaping the persecution and suspicion that surrounded the Shireburns of Stonyhurst, the Daltons of Thurnham, the Heskeths of Rufford and many others.

The buildings, entered through a battlemented gatehouse, are grouped around two courtyards and the state rooms that visitors see occupy the upper or inner courtyard. Originally there was a central tower between the outer and inner courtyards, but this was blown up when the house was captured by the Parliamentary forces in 1643; whether by accident or design is unknown. In the 18th century the house was abandoned when the family moved to Walton-le-Dale, and fell into disrepair. During this period it was sub-let to families of spinners and calico printers, but in the 1870's Sir Henry de Hoghton began a programme of restoration which was completed by the turn of the century, and the house recovered its earlier splendours.

Visitors tour the King's Bedchamber, the Audience Chamber, Ballroom, Banqueting Hall and the other state rooms, noted for their furniture and fine panelling. Of particular interest is the Banqueting Hall which contains its original fireplace and the table at which James I knighted the loin of beef during his stay at Hoghton in 1617. Incidentally, the knighting of the loin was probably done in jest because the king was so delighted with the hospitality he received, and it is not the origin of the word 'sirloin', which comes from the French word *surlonge*. The cost of entertaining the king and his huge retinue almost bankrupted Sir Richard de Hoghton who was forced to spend some time in a debtors prison afterwards.

Other items of interest are the Tudor Well House with its horse-drawn pump, stone cells, dungeons, underground passages, exhibition of historic documents and collection of dolls and dolls houses. In addition there are attractive grounds and walled gardens.

There is a regular bus service between Hoghton and Blackburn which drops you at the gates to Witton Country Park. Details from Blackburn Tourist Information Office (0254 53277).

Spring daffodils at Rufford Old Hall

21. RUFFORD OLD HALL

Start and Finish: Rufford
Distance: 4 miles   *Approximate Time:* 2 hours
Ordnance Survey Landranger Map: 108
Parking: Rufford Old Hall
Refreshments: Tea room at Rufford Old Hall
General Description
Using the half-timbered Rufford Old Hall as a focal point, this is a walk of wide horizons that takes you along the banks of the placid River Douglas and the towpath of the Leeds-Liverpool Canal to cross part of Lancashire's fenland - the intensively farmed reclaimed marshes of the West Lancashire coastal plain.

Route Directions
From the village centre walk down Station Road (signposted Parbold), past the Victorian church, and cross in turn the canal, railway and River Douglas. Just past the bridge over the river, turn left through a gate and walk along the top of the embankment. Go under the railway bridge and continue above the riverbank to a stile. All around are

extensive views across flat, cultivated farmland that was formerly infertile marsh and moss. Climb the stile and soon afterwards turn right down the embankment and follow the grassy strip separating two fields up to a footbridge over a drainage channel. Cross the footbridge, turn left and then right and, where the drain makes a sharp turn to the left, carry on straight ahead towards the railway embankment.

Cross the railway and continue to the next field where you turn left, over a narrow drain and carry on along the edge of the field with a wire fence on the left, keeping roughly parallel with the railway. Over to the right are wide views across the almost treeless expanse of Croston Moss. Cross a plank over the next drain, keep on and follow the edge of the field around to the right to join a straight, wide farm track. Turn left, follow the track to the railway line, cross it and turn right along another straight track. At a crossroad of tracks turn left in front of the farmhouse, and at the next junction bear right and follow the track up to the road. Turn left over the bridge, called Great Hanging Bridge, to cross the River Douglas again and follow the road for 0.75 mile down to the canal bridge. In front are views across Martin Mere, an area of intensive arable cultivation that was once a large lake 18 miles in circumference. The present lake at the Martin Mere Wildfowl Trust nearby is much smaller, and man-made.

At the bridge turn right down to the towpath, left under the bridge and follow the towpath back to Rufford (about 1 mile). The Leeds-Liverpool Canal was constructed between 1770 and 1816 and was 127 miles in length, the longest single canal in Britain. It was built to allow

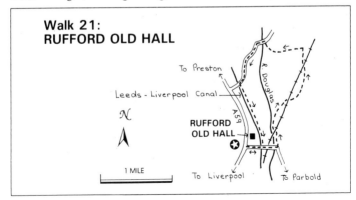

Walk 21:
RUFFORD OLD HALL

To Preston

Leeds - Liverpool Canal

R. Douglas

A59

N

RUFFORD
OLD HALL

1 MILE

To Liverpool   To Parbold

movement of trade across the Pennines between the woollen industries of Yorkshire and the cotton industries of Lancashire and, in particular, to give the area around Leeds access to the port of Liverpool. This branch of it, the Rufford Branch or Douglas Navigation, built in 1805 to provide a link between the main canal and the Ribble estuary, runs roughly parallel with the River Douglas, joining it at Tarleton. It is a pleasant and easy stroll along the towpath with views of Parbold Hill, the most westerly spur of the Pennines, on the horizon. On approaching Rufford the old hall can be seen through the trees on the right. Retrace your steps to the village centre and turn right along the A59 to the main entrance.

Rufford Old Hall

The well-wooded lands of the western marches (North Shropshire, Cheshire and West Lancashire), were lacking in stone for building but possessed an abundance of timber. As a result these areas are especially noted for their black and white half-timbered houses and Rufford is one of the finest of these.

Rufford Old Hall was the home of the Heskeths, another of those Lancashire families who rejected the Protestant religion and remained true to the Catholic Church at the time of the Reformation. The original hall was built as a timber-framed structure on a stone base by Robert Hesketh in the late 15th century. A brick extension was added in 1662 and another addition, in the early 19th century, joined together the 15th and 17th century buildings. By that time, however, the Heskeths had moved out into a new hall across the park, now used as a hospital and separated from the old hall by the busy A59. The Heskeths were an enterprising family and, along with other local landowners, played a prominent role in the reclamation schemes of the 18th and 19th centuries that transformed much of the surrounding area of marshland and barren mosses into one of the most productive vegetable growing regions in the country.

Inside, the most outstanding feature is the Great Hall, built between 1463 and 1490 and one of the best of its kind. It is noted for its magnificent hammerbeam roof, similar in design and construction to the well-known one above Westminster Hall. In addition there are fine collections of paintings, antique furniture and armour and, almost inevitable in a Catholic house, a priest's hiding place. The 19th century block houses a folk museum. A further attraction are the ornamental gardens that lead from the house down to the banks of the canal.

In 1936 Lord Hesketh gave the Hall to the National Trust who have administered it ever since.

Classical elegance - The south front of Lyme Hall

22. LYME PARK

Start and Finish: Lyme Park
Distance: 5.5 miles   *Approximate Time:* 3 hours
Ordnance Survey Landranger Map: 109
Parking: Lyme Park
Refreshments: Restaurant in Lyme Hall

General Description
The bleak moorlands of the Dark Peak clip the north-eastern edge of Cheshire and reach down into Greater Manchester. This walk, no-where more than 6 miles from the centre of Stockport and entirely within or on the boundary of a deer park, has a ruggedness reminiscent of the remoter parts of the Pennines. The views are extensive and varied and at the end there is a magnificent house and its formal gardens to enjoy and explore, a complete contrast to the surrounding wild terrain.

Route Directions
The 1,323 acres of Lyme Park were enclosed as a deer park from the

surrounding Macclesfield Forest in 1346. It is still a deer park today and you will almost certainly see some of the herd during the walk. From the car park take the stepped path up to the entrance to the hall, turn left and walk up the grassy slopes of the hill ahead to the prominent landmark of The Cage. This was built in Elizabethan times as a viewing platform for the hunt and was partially reconstructed in the 18th century. The scene from it today could hardly be more of a contrast - the built-up area of Greater Manchester on one side, and the open moorlands of the Peak District on the other.

At The Cage, turn sharp right (almost doubling back on your tracks) to follow an old fence line downhill and to the left to a tarmac drive. Turn left along the drive and, where it swings right, keep on towards a circle of trees. On approaching the trees bear right and head uphill across rough grass, making for the edge of a wood near the top of the hill. Look out for a ladder-stile in the wall, climb over and follow the path ahead through the wood. A detour of a few yards to the right soon brings you to the Lantern, originally part of the Elizabethan hall and later rebuilt on this spot as a folly.

Climb a ladder-stile at the far end of the wood and turn left to follow the edge of the wall uphill. Where two walls meet, bear right, now following the boundary wall of the park on the left. By now you are quite high up on open moorland and consequently there are extensive views all around: Kinder Scout, Macclesfield Forest domi-

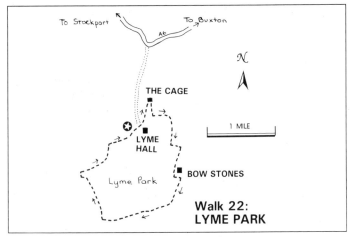

nated by the distinctive shape of Shutlingsloe, Alderley Edge, the Cheshire Plain and Greater Manchester. Follow the wall for just under 0.5 mile and, at a ladder-stile, turn left along a grassy path to another stile which you climb over to join a road. A few yards to the left are the Bow Stones, a group of Anglo-Saxon crosses, or at least the middle portions of them (their heads and bases are elsewhere), possibly placed here in the 16th century as boundary markers.

At the road turn right over a stile and walk along the broad track which gradually draws closer to the boundary wall on the right. After the next stile turn right away from the track (still following the boundary wall), cross another stile and continue, keeping parallel to the wall on the right all the time. On approaching a wire fence in front, bear slightly left, climb a stile and head downhill by a broken wall on the right to a track.

Turn right, passing a cottage on the right, and then left over a stone stile at a public footpath sign to Higher Poynton. There are fine views ahead over the fertile farmland of Cheshire as you cross a field, heading downhill to rejoin the boundary wall of the park. Keep by the wall, above a wooded valley on the right, to a stile. Climb over, continue down to a gate and stile, climb over that and walk down to a road. Turn right in front of a Methodist Church and continue along a track, over a stream and right again through the West Park Gate to re-enter the park.

Follow a track for 0.75 mile through an attractive wooded dell to a gate. Go through and bear right along the tarmac drive back to the car park near the hall.

Lyme Hall

The view of the great house, set in its formal gardens, surrounded by the wooded slopes and bare moorland of the deer park and with its classical facade mirrored in the waters of the pool, is a memorable one. For nearly 600 years it belonged to one family, the Leghs, who enlarged and reconstructed it several times.

Of the original medieval manor house on this site nothing is known but, around the middle of the 16th century, Sir Piers Legh built a large mansion. Large parts of this survive, notably much of the north front (by which visitors approach the hall), the drawing-room and long gallery, the latter containing some superb Elizabethan oak panelling. Further extensions and alterations took place, chiefly in the early 18th century when the Italian architect Leoni built the elegant classical south front (chief feature of the exterior), and again in the early 19th century when Lewis Wyatt re-designed the drawing-room and library and added the tower above the south front.

Inside, your tour includes the great hall (renowned for its 17th century Mortlake tapestries), chapel, saloon, long gallery (already mentioned), bedrooms, library, dining room and drawing-room. All the rooms contain fine paintings, furnishings, wood carvings and tapestries.

Adjoining the house is the orangery and formal gardens, very pleasant and relaxing to wander through after the fairly rough terrain of parts of the walk. There is a Dutch garden, a rose garden, pools and a waterfall and a most attractive terrace garden in front of the orangery.

In 1946 Richard Legh, third Lord Newton, gave both hall and park to the National Trust and it is now administered and maintained by Stockport Council to whom it was leased in 1947.

Harewood House - one of the most sumptuous stately homes in the country

23. HAREWOOD HOUSE

Start and Finish: Harewood House
Distance: 4 miles Approximate Time: 2 hours
Ordnance Survey Landranger Map: 104
Parking: Harewood House
Refreshments: Restaurant and cafe at Harewood House, Harewood Arms in Harewood village

General Description
As well as including some attractive riverside meadows by the Wharfe, this walk is designed to convey something of the evolution of a great country estate. Starting and finishing in landscaped parkland you pass a redundant church, walk through a planned estate village and get distant views of a medieval castle, predecessor of the house that forms the grand finale to the walk. Leave plenty of time at the end to explore thoroughly one of the most sumptuous stately homes in the country, together with its extensive gardens and woodland and other many and varied attractions.

Route Directions

Start by walking back along the drive, away from the house, through the park created in the late 18th century by the best-known landscape architect of the day, Capability Brown. Part of the landscaping involved moving the existing village because it was felt to spoil the view from the house - hence the isolated position and redundant nature of the church, which you can take a look at by making a short detour along the first path on the left by the side of a small plantation.

Returning to the main drive, continue along it and through the main entrance into the village where you turn left. The present Harewood village, obviously purpose-built from its regular and harmonious appearance, was constructed in the late 18th century by John Carr, the same architect who built Harewood House, to replace the earlier village based around the church. The elegant, handsome, well-proportioned cottages are as much a tribute to John Carr's skill as the house itself.

Walk through the village and, just before the main road bends sharply to the left, continue along a broad, clearly-defined track at an Ebor Way public footpath sign. As you proceed downhill there are grand views ahead over the Wharfe valley and the lush, rolling, fertile country of the Vale of York. At the river turn left and keep along the riverbank for 1 mile up to the bridge over the main A61.

Crowning the ridge on the left are the ruins of Harewood Castle, the medieval predecessor of the present house. Paintings of it in the house reveal a once substantial and clearly visible building, but nowadays it is inaccessible to the public and almost hidden by the trees that have grown up around it. It dates from the 12th century but was

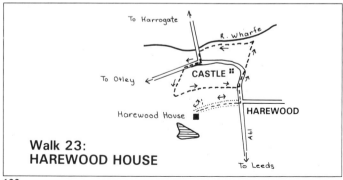

**Walk 23:
HAREWOOD HOUSE**

extensively rebuilt by Sir William de Aldeburgh around the middle of the 14th century and, partly because of this later rebuilding, was more elaborate and less austere than most medieval castles. After being abandoned in the 17th century it was used as a quarry - hence its present sorry and ruinous condition.

At the bridge turn left along the road, right at the T-junction and, after 0.25 mile, left at a public bridleway sign on to a tarmac track to re-enter Harewood Park. The track winds uphill across the rolling parkland studded with trees and on the right is a good view of the prominent, thickly-wooded Rawden Hill. At a junction of tracks turn left and follow the broad, straight drive back to Harewood village, a distance of 1 mile. Turn right along the main road and right again to retrace your steps along the main drive to the house.

Harewood House

A noble and dignified palatial structure, set high upon a ridge above the Wharfe valley from where it surveys its extensive gardens and parkland, Harewood must surely rank as one of the half-dozen or so grandest houses in England. Something of the history and development of the estate will already have been acquired from the walk - the medieval castle, destruction of the old village and building of the new village which is roughly contemporary with the house.

After passing through many owners the estate was acquired by Henry Lascelles in 1739. Exactly twenty years later his son Edwin, who later became the first Lord Harewood in 1790, began the building of the house. Its size and opulence is a reflection of the Lascelles' family wealth, chiefly amassed through the profits of trade with the West Indies, as are the names of the men that were employed in its construction. The list sounds like a roll-call of the greatest craftsmen of the day - John Carr was the architect, Robert Adam designed the interior, Thomas Chippendale (a local man from Otley) made the furniture and, when the house was finished, Capability Brown landscaped the park. Apart from some 19th century changes by Sir Charles Barry (notably the terraces, balconies and a third storey), the house remains substantially the late 18th century creation of Carr and Adam.

Inside, as you might expect, the house is a vast treasure-store possessing, as well as Adam's distinctive decor, a large number of paintings (including some Turner, El Greco and Reynolds), antiques and, of course, Chippendale furniture. Visitors tour the complete circuit of the ground floor state-rooms beginning with the cool and elegant Entrance Hall. Unlike most other houses Harewood boasts not the one library but three - the Old Library (cosy and comfortable-looking), the Spanish Library (so-called because the walls are covered with 17th century Spanish leather) and the Library (part of Barry's 19th century remodelling to accommodate the overflow of books). All are magnificent rooms. Other rooms on the tour include bedrooms, dressing rooms, sitting rooms, the Rose and Green Drawing-rooms, the fine 76 foot Long Gallery, the Dining Room and Music Room, the latter ingeniously creating a circular impression despite being a square-shaped room.

From the formal terraced gardens there are grand views over the gardens, lake and park - a scene that, by looking at some of the paintings inside the house, does not seem to have changed much over the last 200 years. A walk around the ground is definitely rewarding - there is a woodland garden, a rock garden, a rose garden and the additional attractions of the bird garden (approached through the stable block) and, for families with young children, an adventure playground.

Harewood House is still owned and lived in by the Earl and Countess of Harewood.

The Great House Barn, Rivington

24. RIVINGTON

Start and Finish: Rivington (Great House Barn - on the road through Lever Park from Rivington to Horwich)
Distance: 4 miles   *Approximate Time:* 2 hours
Ordnance Survey Landranger Map: 109
Parking: Great House Barn
Refreshments: Great House Barn, Hall Barn and Rivington Hall

General Description
Despite its short length this is an energetic walk, through a fascinating area that embraces a surprisingly varied range of scenery: wooded parkland, open grassland, ornamental gardens, rugged moorland and views over reservoirs and farmland. The historic attractions are even more varied: two ancient barns, Tudor church, 18th century chapel, Georgian mansion and a 20th century reconstruction of a ruined medieval castle.

Rivington

For many centuries Rivington was the centre of a small rural community typical of hundreds found all over England. In the village centre the 16th century parish church and plain but attractive Unitarian chapel (built in 1703) face each other across the green. Nearby stands the 18th century hall, former home of the local landowners, the Pilkington family. Outwardly the village still presents a largely traditional and unchanged appearance that obscures the total transformation of the area that occurred around the turn of the century, the result of the work of a very dynamic and remarkable man.

William Hesketh Lever, later the first Lord Leverhulme, was born in Bolton in 1851. His career as a successful business tycoon began when, as a young man, he leased a small soapworks in Warrington. Soon he built it up into a thriving national company. As his soap empire expanded he established a new factory on the Wirral and around it he built a model estate for his workers called Port Sunlight, planned on similar principles to the Bournville estate that the Cadbury's created for their workers in Birmingham. His philanthropy was not to end there for in 1900, by now a millionaire, he bought the Rivington estate and decided to convert it into a public park for the enjoyment of the people of his native town. An area of rainy and windswept moorland on the western slopes of the Pennines was thus transformed into the landscaped, wooded parkland of Lever Park. Broad straight drives were constructed, trees planted, the two ancient barns restored (unfortunately in a rather insensitive manner), a zoo was set up and, on a ridge above Lower Rivington Reservoir, (originally created in the middle of the 19th century to provide water for the city of Liverpool),

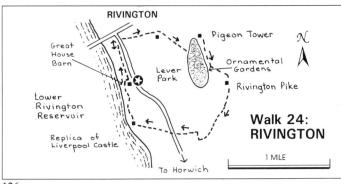

a supposed replica of the medieval ruins of Liverpool Castle was built.

The only private section of Lever Park was the ornamental terraced gardens that Lord Leverhulme created for his personal enjoyment on the lower slopes of Rivington Pike. They were laid out in the Japanese style with lakes, fountains and waterfalls, and near the top he built a wooden bungalow in mock-Tudor style. This was burnt down by suffragettes in 1913 while he and his wife were dining with King George V at nearby Knowsley Hall, though it was later rebuilt in stone.

After Lord Leverhulme's death in 1925 the park became overgrown, the terraced gardens reverted to a wilderness and the bungalow fell into ruin and was eventually demolished. However the area was later taken over by Lancashire County Council as a Country Park and has subsequently been cleared and tidied up, footpaths have been restored and once again the park is fully available for public enjoyment, as its founder intended.

Route Directions

This is an easy route to follow as all the footpaths are clearly marked. From the car park at Great House Barn, one of the two ancient barns and now used as a cafe and Country Park Information Centre, follow the waymarked footpath on the left, that runs roughly parallel with the road, to Rivington village. It is a pleasant and easy stroll of about 0.25 mile across wooded grassland and by a stream, the path joins the road near the village green. In the village, take a look at the parish church and small Unitarian chapel before retracing your steps a few yards along the road and bearing left along the broad straight track up to Hall Barn. This is the larger of the two cruck barns that may be of Saxon origin. Nowadays, as a result of Lord Leverhulme's restoration, both of them look like typical Victorian mock-Tudor structures and Hall Barn serves as a licensed restaurant. By the side of it is the 18th century Rivington Hall, former home of the lords of the manor and also used as a restaurant. There is no way in which you can go hungry around Rivington.

Go straight past Hall Barn and take the path at the back of it. Follow the path to the left, climb a stile, continue straight on and climb another stile to enter the wooded terraced gardens, former private grounds of Lord Leverhulme. At this stage there is little point in giving precise instructions as there is a myriad of footpaths and it is a pleasure just to wander through the gardens, up steps and under arches, without worrying too much about where you are going. All you need to remember is to keep ascending and ultimately make for the prominent landmark of the Pigeon Tower, built by Lord Leverhulme as a dovecote, at the top left-hand corner of the gardens.

From the Pigeon Tower there are extensive views over the reservoirs and surrounding moorland. Turn right along the broad track at the back of the tower and bear left along the equally broad track that ascends Rivington Pike. It is quite a steep climb to the summit, nearly 1,200 feet high, but well worth the effort for the views from the top are breathtaking. To the south and west the reservoirs look like a miniature Lake District and beyond them lies the flat farmland of the coastal plain. To the north and east are contrasting views across the bleak and bare Rivington and Anglezarke Moors, with the Winter Hill television transmitter most prominent on the skyline. On clear days the mountains of North Wales and Cumbria can be seen. Rivington Pike was used as a warning beacon during national emergencies, like the coming of the Spanish Armada in 1588, and the tower on top was built in 1773.

Bear right and follow the path down from the summit. At the wire fence turn right through a gate and continue downhill along the clear broad track. Over to the left the houses on the edge of Horwich can be seen. Where the track swings to the left, turn right along another wide track and, at the end of the railings on the left, turn left and follow the path down through the trees by the edge of school grounds and buildings. At the road turn right and shortly afterwards bear left along the bridleway (signposted Castle) that leads straight as a dye to the mock ruins of the replica Liverpool Castle.

The original castle stood in the centre of Liverpool but there is nothing left of it. Why Lord Leverhulme wanted to build a sham ruin of it here is something of a puzzle, but he was probably indulging in a rich man's fantasy for creating something romantic. Nowadays it looks more forlorn than romantic, but it occupies a fine site above Lower Rivington Reservoir and from its walls there are excellent views across the parkland to the Pike, with both towers clearly visible on the horizon. At the castle turn right and follow the path that runs parallel with the reservoir (railings on the left) back to Great House Barn.

HERITAGE OF THE FORESTS

Forests conjure up an image of large wooded expanses, scattered glades and open heathland in which outlaws in Lincoln green used to lurk and over which king and nobles used to hunt the deer. As far as the forests of the north-west are concerned, only the latter is true.

In the Middle Ages a forest was any piece of land set aside as a hunting ground for the king, whether it was extensively wooded or not, and could include mountain and moorland, arable land and marshes, villages and even small towns. The forests of the north-west always comprised predominantly open moorland, far removed from the more conventional and perhaps better known forests of the midlands and the south. In Lancashire the forests of Rossendale, Trawden, Pendle and Bowland formed an almost unbroken and continuous hunting area stretching from the Irwell to the Lune, and from the western slopes of the Pennines to the Irish Sea coast. Despite the later industrialisation and urbanisation of much of this area they still retain a perhaps surprising amount of open, lonely, wild and unspoilt country.

The following walks explore two parts of the Forest of Bowland, both on its southern fringes overlooking the beautiful Hodder valley. Overlooking Bowland from the other side of the Ribble valley lies the brooding mass of Pendle Hill, indelibly associated with the witch trials of the early 17th century. Here we follow a 'Pendle Witches' trail.

The Hark-to-Bounty at Slaidburn

25. FOREST OF BOWLAND

Start and Finish: Slaidburn
Distance: 4 miles   *Approximate Time:* 2 hours
Ordnance Survey Landranger Map: 103
Parking: Slaidburn
Refreshments: Hark to Bounty at Slaidburn, cafe and Parkers Arms at Newton

General Description

The wild and lonely Forest of Bowland provides some of the finest scenery in the north of England. This short walk, which starts and finishes in one of the most picturesque villages in Lancashire, has superb views and includes a particularly lovely stretch of the River Hodder.

Slaidburn and the Forest of Bowland

We usually think of a forest as a large thickly-wooded region, but the bare and open uplands and lush river-pastures of Bowland do not fit that description at all. In fact in medieval times a forest was any piece of land that was reserved for the king as a royal hunting ground and protected by a special and additional code of laws. Usually such areas were a mixture of woodland and heath, like the traditional New and Sherwood forests, but in the north and west moorland areas like Exmoor, Dartmoor, the High Peak, Rossendale and Bowland also served that purpose. The Forest of Bowland undoubtedly possessed more trees in the Middle Ages than now, but it would never have been extensively wooded.

To complicate matters it was not originally a forest but a chase. A chase was a private as opposed to a royal hunting ground, and before 1066 Bowland belonged to Earl Tostig of Northumbria, brother of the unfortunate King Harold. Tostig was banished from his earldom and in 1066 attempted to regain it in alliance with the King of Norway. Both Tostig and the Norwegian king were killed at the battle of Stamford Bridge, just a few weeks before Harold's own defeat and death at Hastings. Following the Norman Conquest the Forest of Bowland became part of the 'Honour of Clitheroe', the vast estates that belonged to the de Lacys, Lords of Clitheroe Castle. In 1311 these estates passed by marriage to Thomas Earl of Lancaster and, when the then Duke of Lancaster ascended the throne in 1399 as King Henry IV, Bowland became one of the 90 or so royal forests. By this time royal forests were on the decline and parts of Bowland were beginning to be enclosed and turned into farmland. Most of the area was disafforested during the 17th century and sold to various private owners.

Slaidburn was the main administrative centre of Bowland and its most tangible surviving link with the days of the royal forest and forest laws is the courtroom attached to the Hark to Bounty Inn, where the forest courts used to hold their regular meetings. The village, occupying a pleasant situation above the River Hodder, comprises a number of attractive 18th century cottages, an old grammar school building (built and endowed by John Brennand in 1717) and a medieval church founded in the 12th century, but mainly dating from the 15th century.

Route Directions

From the village centre take the lane past the Hark to Bounty and follow it uphill out of the village. After passing some farm buildings on the left, turn left through a metal gate and follow the broad stony track ahead as it winds its way across Pain Hill Moor. All around are superb and extensive views over the Pennines, Bowland Fells and Hodder Valley. Keep along the track through a farmyard, turn right at the house, then left and continue with a stone wall on your left. Soon you see a farmhouse in front. Go through a gate in a wall to the farmhouse and carry on along the farm track to the lane. Turn left, and with glorious views over the Hodder Valley to Waddington and Easington Fells beyond, walk downhill into the village of Newton passing on the left the Quaker Meeting House. Turn left at the road.

Newton is little more than a hamlet lying astride the main route through Bowland from Clitheroe to Lancaster. John Paslew, last abbot of Whalley, travelled this way in 1537 to his trial and execution at Lancaster Castle, as did the Pendle witches just over half a century later.

The Quaker Meeting House, dated 1767, is an interesting reminder of how the Quakers, founded by George Fox around the middle of the 17th century, were forced to seek remote places because of unpopularity. Their unorthodox views and informal services caused them to be regarded with suspicion, not only by the established Church of England, but also by other Nonconformist sects. Accordingly they often built their places of worship in out of the way villages, and Newton was ideal. At one time there was a Quaker school here, attended in his teenage years by the noted 19th century reformer John Bright.

The route back to Slaidburn is mostly along the banks of the Hodder. Proceed through the village following signposts to Clitheroe and, just before the bridge, turn left through a gate (public footpath

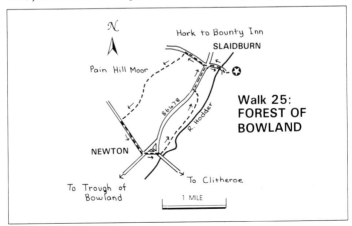

sign to Slaidburn) to take the riverside path. Carry on to another gate and where the river bends to the right, cross a footbridge and keep straight on by a wall on the right. Go through a gate in the wall, turn left across the field keeping parallel to the wall and fence on the left, and shortly rejoin the meandering Hodder at the base of the wooded Great Dunnow Hill. Keep along the path between river and hill, through a gate on the left, ahead and through another gate.

Across the riverside meadows to the right the farm buildings of the hamlet of Easington can be seen, and in front you catch a glimpse of Dunnow Hall. Soon you bear left to join a main path coming from the footbridge over the river and, still skirting the base of the steep wooded hill, follow it through a metal gate and up to the Newton-Slaidburn road. Turn right, and with a good view of Slaidburn church in front, follow the road back to the village.

Browsholme Hall in the Forest of Bowland

26. BROWSHOLME HALL

Start and Finish: Whitewell
Distance: 4.5 miles **Approximate Time: 2hrs 30 mins**
Ordnance Survey Landranger Map: 103
Parking: Just beside the church and hotel at Whitewell
Refreshments: Inn at Whitewell
General Description
Starting and finishing at Whitewell, an exceptionally attractive spot in the wooded Hodder Valley, this walk climbs out of the valley and takes you across fields and over hillsides to a fine Tudor mansion. All the way there are sweeping and, at times, dramatic views across the open and lonely expanses of the Bowland Fells.

Route directions (Whitewell to Browsholme Hall)
The thickly-wooded and steep-sided valley of the Hodder around Whitewell has been justifiably compared with Switzerland. Whitewell is little more than a hamlet comprising a small church, built in 1818 on the site of a medieval chapel, and an attractive, rambling inn, built on the site of a medieval manor house. Parts of the inn date back to the

Middle Ages and it was once the home of royal foresters and the meeting place of the Swainmotes, the local forest courts for Bowland.

Start by walking up the lane opposite the hotel and, after about 100 yards, turn right up some steps and through a gate into a field. Keep straight on, passing the right-hand side of a farm, turn left in front of the farm and continue uphill towards a metal gate, keeping roughly parallel to a line of trees on the left. Immediately you are confronted by superb views over the Bowland Fells - a characteristic of most of this walk. Go through the gate and keep on, skirting the side of a hill on the right to rejoin the lane at a gate.

Cross over and through the metal gate opposite, heading across the field to a ladder-stile and keeping roughly parallel with the lane. Climb over and keep ahead veering slightly to the left. Continue climbing, passing a prominent circle of trees in front, up to a wall. Look for a stile in the wall which enables you to climb over, then climb over a stile in a wire fence immediately in front, into a conifer plantation. Follow the path through the middle of the plantation and, emerging from the trees, turn left over a stile, sharp right by the wire fence on the right (which is the plantation boundary) and bear slightly left towards a broken wall. Go through, across a brook and continue by a wire fence on the right, making for a farmhouse in front. Keeping to the right of the farm, climb a stile, go down some steps and turn right along the farm track to the road.

At the road, which is on the line of a Roman road between the forts

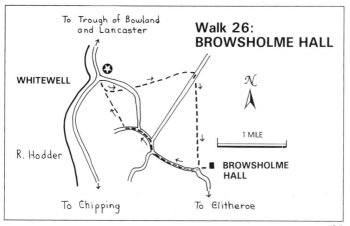

135

of Ribchester and Ilkley, turn right and almost immediately left over a stile in a wire fence. Turn right and head uphill across rough grassland, gradually drawing away from the road on the right towards a stile in the wire fence ahead. Climb over, turn left along the edge of the fence and, where the fence ends, walk on in the direction of the farmhouse in front, crossing a farm track and joining a wire fence on the right that borders a plantation. Climb a stile and keep on squeezing between a fence on the right and wall on the left. At the end of the wall continue ahead, and climb another stile in the fence near the right-hand side of the farm.

Now you head across a large field, veering away from the fence on the right and towards the far end of a line of trees on the left, where you follow a wire fence around to the left to a stile. Climb over, turn right and make for the left-hand side of a group of trees in front. Cross over a stile, continue by the edge of the trees to another stile, and head across the middle of the next field in the direction of a farm track clearly visible in front. Go through a gate and along the track, through a gate at the end and turn left up to the hall.

Browsholme Hall
Standing in a fine position on the south-western fringes of the Forest of Bowland, Browsholme Hall is, despite later additions and reconstructions, still basically the Tudor mansion first built by Edmund Parker in 1507. It has the distinction of having been occupied by the same family throughout its history, a family, moreover, with close connections with the forest. From the 16th century onwards the Parkers were hereditary bowbearers or wardens of the Forest of Bowland, which means that they were the king's chief agent responsible for the administration of the forest and the enforcement of forest laws.

The original Tudor house was extended and the frontage refaced by Thomas Parker in the early 17th century. Further reconstructions and additions took place in the early 18th century, and again in the early 19th century when Jeffry Wyatt built a new dining room and rebuilt the west wing. Externally the most impressive feature is the long Elizabethan facade, built of local sandstone. Inside the state-rooms contain family portraits, furniture, arms, armour and stained glass. The major rooms are the Tudor hall, library (walled-off from the hall in 1754 and with 17th century panelling brought from another house in 1809), drawing-room and dining room (both part of Wyatt's 19th century changes) and the attractive oak drawing-room with its early 18th century panelling.

The overall impression of Browsholme is of a homely and unpretentious rather than grand stately house; perhaps a reflection both of continuous family occupation and a comparatively remote situation.

Route Directions (Brownsholme Hall to Whitewell)

Return to the road turn right and follow it for 0.75 mile, bearing left into the hamlet of Cow Ark. Here you turn right (along the road signposted to Whitewell via Hall Hill and Newton) and follow it for a further 0.5 mile before turning left along a farm road signposted to Radholme Laund, (laund refers to a lawn or open space in the forest used for grazing). Go through the farmyard and, just after passing the large house on the left, turn right and go through a gate into the field ahead, keeping by the wall on your right.

When you reach the brow of the hill you get the most magnificent views of the entire walk unfolding in front, and staying with you the rest of the way. The Hodder winds below and the rounded outlines of the fells stretch away towards the Trough of Bowland in the distance. Over the brow make for a metal gate in front. Go through it, bearing half-right across the field to another metal gate at the corner of the wall, go through that, turn left and follow the edge of the next field (wall on the left). Keep on through another gate and head downhill by a wall on the left. Near the bottom corner of the field climb a stile in the wall ahead and continue downhill, passing the left-hand side of the farmhouse, to a gate in the fence. Go down the steps and turn left along the lane back into Whitewell.

Pendle Hill broods over the village of Barley

27. PENDLE WITCH COUNTRY

Start and Finish: Barley
Distance: 5 miles   *Approximate Time:* 2hrs 30 mins
Ordnance Survey Landranger Map: 103
Parking: Barley Picnic Area
Refreshments: Pubs in Barley, Roughlee and Newchurch, snacks at the Barley Picnic Area, cafe at Newchurch

General Description

This walk takes you through the heart of the witch country around Pendle, linking the attractive villages of Barley, Roughlee and Newchurch. There are splendid views all the way, dominated inevitably by the brooding giant of Pendle Hill itself.

Pendle and the Witches

The name Pendle comes from the Celtic 'pen' meaning hill, a word familiar in nearby Pen-y-ghent, but more frequently found in Wales. In medieval times the Pendle area, though largely treeless as now, was a forest and wild boar were hunted there as late as the 17th century. With its distinctive outline and bare, sometimes forbidding appearance, Pendle Hill provides an appropriate setting for witchcraft stories, its frequent cloud-cover giving it an air of mystery and danger.

The trial of the Pendle Witches took place in 1612 and was one of several at the time. James I had written a book on witchcraft while King of Scotland and his accession to the English throne in 1603 inaugurated a period of witch purges. It was a highly superstitious age in which any simple-minded old woman who perhaps talked to herself and had eccentric habits might be suspected of being a witch. Two such women in the Pendle area were Annie Whittle and Elizabeth Southerns, nicknamed Chattox and Old Demdike respectively. The trouble seems to have originated as the result of a feud between them that began when Chattox's daughter broke into Demdike's home and stole some clothes. The matter was reported to the local magistrate, Roger Nowell of Read Hall, who carried out an investigation during which several people made allegations of witchcraft against both women, and some of their families. Under interrogation the simple and ignorant old women not surprisingly confessed to their alleged crimes and were sent for trial at Lancaster Castle. After a meeting of the various families at Demdike's house, Malkin Tower, the site of which is unknown, several others were accused and sent to Lancaster, including Alice Nutter of Roughlee Hall. Why such a woman of means, from a totally different social environment, should have been consorting with these rougher and poorer elements has always been a mystery.

At the trial charges against the accused included desecrating bodies, turning beer sour and hastening someone's death. The women were too ignorant to defend themselves and the verdict was a foregone conclusion. In August 1612 nine of the Pendle Witches were hanged outside Lancaster Castle, though not Old Demdike, she had died before the opening of the trial.

Information about the trial comes from the pen of Thomas Potts, clerk to the judge, who published a book in 1613 called *The Wonderful Discovery of Witches in the County of Lancaster*. Over the following centuries stories of the Pendle Witches spread throughout the country and beyond, boosted considerably by the novels of Harrison Ainsworth *The Lancashire Witches* (1848) and Robert Neill *Mist Over Pendle* (1951). Nowadays the witches have become the focal point of a flourishing tourist industry.

Route Directions

From the picnic area in Barley head towards the mill chimney, follow the path between the mill buildings and cottages and then along the left bank of Pendle Water. At the footbridge keep on through a gate, continue along the bank of the stream over two stiles and, at the second stile, turn left to climb steeply through a small wood. At the top climb a stile and head across the field to another stile in a gap in the hedge. Bearing slightly to the left, walk in a straight line across five fields (stiles easily visible in front). When you reach the last field next to a caravan site, make for the far right-hand corner of it, climb the stile and turn right down the lane into Roughlee. Just before the road junction turn left in front of some houses and follow the path for a few yards to Roughlee Hall.

The hall is on the left and is a fine 17th century building. It was the home of Alice Nutter, the odd one out among the Pendle Witches. Nowadays it is divided into a number of separate cottages.

Turn right past the hall, right again at the road and, in the centre of Roughlee, turn left over the bridge and take the steep uphill road to Barrowford. At the top of the hill make a sharp turn to the right and follow a wide tarmac track, soon passing the wall of Kidgaling Reservoir on the left. All around are extensive views with Blacko Tower standing out prominently. At the end of the reservoir wall bear slightly to the right along another straight track (wire fence on left, hedge on right). Where the track enters a field and swings to the right keep straight on by a wall on the left to come out onto a lane near a cafe.

Continue along the lane for a few yards and, at a public footpath sign, turn right and head diagonally across the field to the corner of a wall on the left. Follow the wall round to the left, making for a gate directly ahead, go through and keep on to another gate. At this point

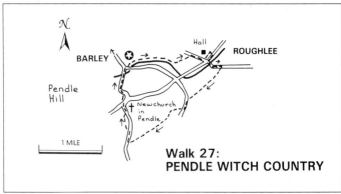

Walk 27:
PENDLE WITCH COUNTRY

there is no clear path but the television transmitter in front acts as a convenient landmark. Keeping in direct line with the transmitter climb several stiles, and after passing a farm on the left cross a stile in a wire fence and make for the right-hand corner of the wall ahead. To the right the cottages and church of Newchurch stand out clearly on the hillside, with the houses of Spen Brook in the valley below.

At the corner of the wall walk on along a track, past another farm on the right and onto the road. Turn right and head downhill, soon bearing left along a clear footpath towards Newchurch. Climb over the gap between a fence and the corner of a wall, keep straight on and at the road turn left uphill to enter the attractive village of Newchurch-in-Pendle.

There was no church in the Pendle area until the building of the 'new church' here in 1544. It was mainly rebuilt in the 18th century and its distinguishing feature is the gap in the stonework near the base of the tower called the 'Eye of God'. At the trial of the Pendle Witches in 1612 some of them were accused of desecrating corpses in Newchurch graveyard.

In the centre of the village take the steep uphill path to the left of the public conveniences, and follow it through two gates. At the top bear slightly to the right to a stile. Climb over, turn left and follow the road downhill for 0.5 mile back to Barley.

LITERARY HERITAGE

All over the country there are shrines besieged every year by ever-increasing numbers of a new type of pilgrim, people who like to visit places associated with great literary figures and try to absorb something of the atmosphere of the surroundings that inspired their writings. Here in the north-west are two of the most popular of these literary shrines.

Without the Brontës, Haworth would presumably, still be a rather remote and largely unknown Pennine hill village. This remarkable trio of sisters were the daughters of the local parson and, despite their comparatively sheltered existence and short lives, produced works of great passion and intensity that have become among the foremost treasures of English literature. The parsonage is now a Brontë museum and nearby in their father's former church, most of the family are buried.

Wordsworth is undoubtedly England's best-known poet, both at home and abroad; even the least 'poetic' of people can usually recite two lines from *Daffodils* if nothing else! Most of his life was spent in his beloved Lake District, especially around Grasmere and Rydal, and his poetry played a major role in attracting some of the first tourists into the area. Both villages possess houses in which he lived and worked; adjoining Dove Cottage at Grasmere is a well-stocked Wordsworth museum.

More than most writers, both the Brontës and Wordsworth were deeply influenced by their scenic environment and the following walks seek to introduce you to each of those very different environments. The first takes you across the bleak and rugged moors around Haworth to the supposed setting of *Wuthering Heights*. The second is a classic Wordsworth walk around the lakes of Grasmere and Rydal Water, the country most familiar to him.

Grasmere Sports in Edwardian days Photo: Abbot Hall Gallery, Kendal

28. WORDSWORTH COUNTRY

Start and Finish: Grasmere
Distance: 5 miles   *Approximate Time:* 2hrs 30 mins
Ordnance Survey Landranger Map : 90
Parking: Grasmere
Refreshments: Pubs, cafés and restaurants in Grasmere

General Description
Despite being surrounded by high fells this is an easy walk around the adjoining lakes of Grasmere and Rydal Water in the heart of 'Wordsworth Country'. Two of the poets residences are passed, as well as the churchyard in which he lies buried. This is very much a lakeside and woodland walk, possibly at its best in October when the trees are in their autumn finery.

Route Directions (Grasmere to Dove Cottage)
From the village centre walk along Stock Lane past the church to the

Ambleside-Keswick road. Cross over, take the lane opposite and Dove Cottage is a few yards along on the left.

Wordsworth and Dove Cottage

Most of Wordsworth's life revolved around and was spent in his native Lake District. Born at Cockermouth in 1770, he went to school in Hawkshead and then on to university at Cambridge. After journeying around England and France (where he became a keen supporter of the revolution), plus brief stays in Dorset and Somerset, he returned to Cumbria in 1799. He moved into Dove Cottage at Grasmere, originally a 17th century inn called the 'Dove and Olive - Bough', with his sister Dorothy and lived there for the next nine years. They were probably the happiest and most productive years in his life.

In 1802 he married Mary Hutchinson, a local girl whom he had known for many years, and three of his children were born there. Some of his best-known poetry was written at Dove Cottage and while there he entertained a number of distinguished literary contemporaries such as Coleridge, Southey, de Quincey and Scott.

The only trouble was that the cottage was too small for a growing family and therefore in 1808 the Wordsworths moved to a larger house in Grasmere. His friend and fellow poet de Quincey, took over the tenancy and lived there for the next twenty-seven years. After several other moves Wordsworth eventually settled at Rydal Mount in 1813, where he stayed for the rest of his life.

In 1890 Dove Cottage was given to a Trust who still own it and maintain both the house and garden much as they were in Wordsworth's time. The adjoining Grasmere and Wordsworth Museum, opened in 1981 in a former Victorian coachhouse, has displays of manuscripts, books, photographs and the personal possessions of the poet and his family.

Route Directions (Dove Cottage to Rydal Mount)

Continue up the lane past Dove Cottage and, where it bears right, continue uphill following the track round to the right where it soon flattens out. You now follow a fairly straight, clear and gently undulating path for 1.25 miles to Rydal, partly through attractive woodland and partly across open country, below the steep crags of Nab Scar.

This is a very pleasant route with superb views through the trees over Rydal Water to the right. On approaching some houses turn right at a T-junction and Rydal Mount is immediately on the right.

Rydal Mount

The immediate and most obvious impression is of a much larger and grander house than the comparatively humble Dove Cottage, a reflection of Wordsworth's greater affluence and more established status. He lived here longer than anywhere else, from 1813 until his death in 1850 at the ripe old age of 80, and it is still in the possession of one of his descendants. Inside are many books, pictures and family possessions and the large garden, overlooking Rydal Water, was landscaped by the poet.

Just down the road is Rydal church (built in 1824) and behind it is the wooded hillside of Dora's Field, bought by Wordsworth for his favourite daughter. It is noted for its fine display of daffodils in springtime.

Route Directions (Rydal Mount to Grasmere)

Continue down the lane to the main road. Turn left and soon afterwards right over Pelter Bridge, an old pack-horse bridge across the River Rothay, and right again along the metalled road. After the last houses the road becomes a rough track which continues through woodland, eventually emerging out of the woods on to the open fellside.

At this point the path forks and you have a choice between the lower lakeside and riverside path on the right, and the higher path to the left. For the best views bear left along the higher path, from which you immediately get a superb panoramic view over Rydal Water.

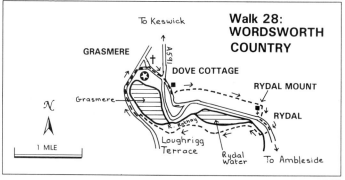

Continue along past caves and old quarries, keeping roughly parallel to the lake (and later the river) below all the way. At the next choice of paths bear slightly to the right along the middle way between the higher path on the left, and the lakeside path on the right. This is the well-known viewpoint of Loughrigg Terrace, from which the view over Grasmere lake and village, backed by Helm Crag, is absolutely magnificent.

Carry on along the easy to follow path but, just before reaching a belt of woodland, head off to the right down one of the steep grassy paths to the lakeside. Turn left and follow the path through the woods, through a gate and across meadows, keeping by the lake all the way. Climb a stile and shortly afterwards the path veers left away from the lake up to a road. Turn right and follow the narrow twisting road for 0.75 mile back to Grasmere. Having seen two of Wordsworth's homes on the walk it would be appropriate to finish off by making your way to the churchyard of Grasmere's simple, plain 13th century church in which the poet and many of his family are buried.

Haworth Parsonage - the Brontë family home

29. BRONTE COUNTRY

Start and Finish: Haworth
Distance: 7 miles   *Approximate time:* 3hrs 30 mins
Ordnance Survey Landranger Maps: 103 and 104
Parking: Haworth
Refreshments: Plenty of pubs, cafés and restaurants in Haworth

General Description
The bleak, heathery moorland to the west of Haworth provides the setting for the literary works of the Brontë sisters. From Haworth the walk takes you across the moors to Top Withens with its associations with *Wuthering Heights*, the most powerfully evocative of all the Brontë novels. Wild though these moors are the well-used paths are clear and easy to follow and the views are magnificent all the way.

Route Directions (Haworth to Top Withens)
From the centre of Haworth take the footpath on the north side of the church, past the parsonage (public footpath sign to Haworth Moor), through a gate and follow the flagged path across fields to the road. Turn left and left again at the first junction (signposted Penistone Hill),

soon after you bear right along a wide grassy track that heads straight for Lower Laithe Reservoir. At the road turn right along the top of the dam wall and, when you reach the Haworth-Colne road, turn left into the village of Stanbury.

Stanbury is a pleaant village of old stone cottages and a tiny church, the wide upper windows of some of the cottages indicate that it was once a handloom weaving village. Go through the village and at the far end turn left (near a bus stop) along a narrow, tarmac lane. Keep on, climbing steadily all the time, following public footpath signs to Brontë Waterfalls and Top Withens. The lane gradually deteriorates into a rough track but you keep straight on and, immediately after going through a gate, bear right at a fork in the track following the signs for Top Withens. Now you are in real Brontë country; all around you is a vast expanse of wild, bleak, treeless, windswept moorland.

You shortly join the Pennine Way, continuing the steady climb and passing on your right Lower and Upper Heights farms. A flight of steps cut into the moorland brings you to Top Withens.

Top Withens
The ruined farmhouse in its moorland setting, battered by winds from all angles, is the reputed setting of *Wuthering Heights*. The actual house could not have been the model as it is far too small and does not fit the description in the book, but it is believed that Emily Brontë may have had the setting in mind. It is certainly a very atmospheric spot with extensive, panoramic views and the house dominates the landscape, even in its ruined state.

Route Directions (Top Withens to Haworth)
Retrace your steps for about 300 yards to another even more ruinous farmhouse and bear right away from your original route to follow a

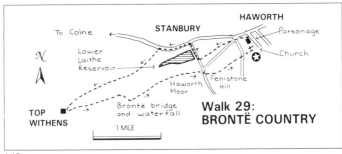

Walk 29:
BRONTË COUNTRY

grassy track downhill. Continue along the track which keeps to the left side of a beck and, soon after reaching a stone wall, climb some steps and carry on ahead before dropping down to the Brontë Bridge and Waterfalls. This is a popular beauty spot and is supposed to have been a favourite resting place for the sisters on their frequent moorland walks.

Cross the bridge and turn left along the broad, well-used track following Brontë Way signs. You pass several ruined farmhouses and over to the left are fine views of Stanbury, and in the distance the buildings of Keighley. On reaching the road turn right for a few yards and then left (public footpath sign to Haworth) across the rough moorland of Penistone Hill Country Park to a car park. Turn left and continue following the signs to Haworth and the yellow waymarks. At a junction of paths turn left down to the road, go straight across and continue downhill along a tree-lined path between stone walls. Turn left onto a flagged path and follow it down to Haworth churchyard. The church is on your right and the parsonage on your left.

Haworth and the Brontës
Nowadays Haworth has become one of Britain's major literary meccas, on a par with Stratford-on-Avon and Grasmere, but in the Middle Ages it was a small, obscure village on the edge of the moors with most of its inhabitants earning their living through farming and quarrying. With the growth of the local woollen industry it later developed, like many Pennine villages, into a centre for handloom weaving. The 18th century was the heyday of the handloom weavers, but the prosperity and population expansion of that era is nothing compared with the tourist boom of recent years since the 'Brontë industry' took off.

It was in 1820 that the Rev. Patrick Brontë, a clergyman of Irish origin, moved to Haworth with his wife and six children and took up residence in the parsonage. Over the next thirty years his family life was to be one long series of tragedies. In 1821 his wife died, followed in 1825 by two of his children, Maria and Elizabeth. Life for the other four; Branwell, Charlotte, Emily and Anne must have been hard in that bleak house with no mother and a father who had little to do with them. In order to occupy themselves in the long winter months they began to invent characters and write stories, early glimmerings of their future literary careers.

Patrick's only son, Branwell, turned out to be a great disappointment. He became a heavy drinker, drifted into a number of jobs from which he was dismissed, began to take opium and died at the early age of 31. Meanwhile the three girls started to enjoy literary success following their first publication, a joint venture, in 1846. Charlotte achieved instant fame with *Jane Eyre* in 1847, Emily's *Wuthering Heights* and Anne's *Agnes Grey* were published in the same year but the former novel, perhaps surprisingly in view of its later success, did not become popular until long after Emily's death in 1848. Anne died in Scarborough in 1849 (the only member of the family not to die and be buried in Haworth), thus leaving only Charlotte with her father in the parsonage. In 1854 a new resident arrived when Charlotte married her father's curate, Arthur Bell Nicholls, but the marriage lasted less than a year for in 1855 Charlotte died. The Rev. Brontë outlived them all, dying in 1861 at the age of 84. All three sisters had died at early ages - Ann (29), Emily (30) and Charlotte (38) - the victims of illnesses brought on by a combination of a harsh climate and damp, unhealthy living conditions.

The parsonage is still basically the same late 18th century house in which they lived and contains much of their original furniture. It is full of fascinating memorabilia - letters, personal belongings etc. - much of which is housed in the 19th century extension built by a later incumbent which comprises an exhibition and library. The house is administered and maintained by the Brontë Society.

There is a fine view of the church from the front of the parsonage, but it is not the same one that the Brontë sisters would have seen. The plain, simple 17th-18th century church of which their father was curate was pulled down and rebuilt in 1861, apart from the tower. Beneath the Brontë chapel, completed in 1964, lies the family vault in which the Rev. Patrick Brontë and all his children, except Anne, are buried. Nearby a display case contains several interesting documents relating to the lives of the family, including Charlotte's marriage certificate

It seems remarkable that these three vicar's daughters living in an obscure village, unmarried (except briefly for Charlotte), having few contacts with the outside world and generally leading the sheltered lives of young Victorian ladies of the times, should have written works of such emotion and passion and become so famous, especially in view of their very short lives. However they did and their tragic lives and books draw thousands of visitors every year to this grey, steep, hilltop village that was their home, and to the wild moors that inspired them.

INDUSTRIAL HERITAGE

Up to the beginning of the 18th century the north-west was one of the most sparsely populated and remote parts of England, with few large towns, poor communications, generally cut off from the mainstream of English history. The advent of the Industrial Revolution changed all that very swiftly and dramatically and the north-west became one of the cradles of the modern technology, and a major pioneer of economic, social and technical innovation.

A combination of fast-flowing streams, coal and iron deposits and proximity to convenient ports, plus transport improvements (first canals and later railways), transformed many parts of the region, especially south Lancashire, west Yorkshire, north Cheshire and west Cumbria, into great industrial areas. Old towns expanded, new towns sprang up almost overnight and thousands of workers flocked into these new industrial towns from the surrounding rural areas. This great outburst of energy and creation transformed the appearance and environment of the north-west to a greater extent than any other single event.

Above all the legacy of small, cottage-based spinning and weaving in the area, on both sides of the Pennines, formed the basis for the development of the area as the country's major textile manufacturing region. From being on the periphery of national events the north-west was thrust into the forefront and many of the great names of England's industrial heritage are north-western ones - Richard Arkwright, Samuel Crompton, Samuel Greg, Sir Titus Salt, Lord Leverhulme, etc.

Both cotton and wool reached their peak in the first decade of the 20th century. Since the First World War however they, along with the other traditional industries and the communications network associated with them have declined, and the area is now undergoing a new era of industrial change, an ever-continuing process. Many vestiges of the 18th and 19th century heyday of those great industries remain - early handloom weaving communities, mills, purpose-built industrial villages, canals, warehouses, and disused railways. The most outstanding of these vestiges are visited during the course of this last group of walks.

Old bridges and ruined Hall at Wycoller

30. WYCOLLER

Start and Finish: Wycoller - about 2 miles south of Colne at end of the minor road from Trawden
Distance: 5 miles   *Approximate Time:* 2hrs 30 mins
Ordnance Survey Landranger Map: 103
Parking: Country Park car park about 0.25 mile from the village
Refreshments: Café in Wycoller

General Description
From the old handloom weavers' village of Wycoller, this walk takes you across fields and along tracks through open country that at one time formed part of the ancient Forest of Trawden. All the way there are magnificent views over Pendle Hill to the north and the edge of the Brontë moors to the south.

Wycoller
Wycoller is one of the most fascinating and attractive of Pennine villages. Its stone buildings occupy an idyllic position in a sheltered,

wooded dene through which flows Wycoller Beck.

The village was originally a small agricultural settlement deep in the Forest of Trawden, one of the many royal forests that in the Middle Ages covered a third of England's total area. The most striking remains of its medieval past are the unique vertical stone slabs that formed the vaccary walls, used to enclose cattle. During the 16th and 17th centuries the forest was gradually thinned out and, with sheep on the nearby moorlands and a plentiful supply of water, Wycoller became a centre of woollen handloom weaving. The invention of water and steam-powered spinning machines during the Industrial Revolution created a boom for the handloom weavers and Wycoller reached the peak of its prosperity about 1820 when its population was around 350. The introduction of the power loom spelt doom for the handloom weavers and this, coupled with the remoteness of the village from the major centres of industry, led to its sharp decline. The population dropped to 231 in 1851, and 107 by 1871. During the present century Wycoller was almost deserted and most of the cottages abandoned and derelict. In 1973 the village and surrounding farms were purchased by Lancashire County Council who created a conservation area and Country Park. Since then there has been a welcome revival. Most of the cottages have been restored and are now inhabited, a craft centre and café have opened and the ruins of the hall have been cleared and made safe.

Wycoller Hall dates from the Tudor period and was the home of the Hartley family. It later passed by marriage to the Cunliffes and, in the late 18th century, it was extended by the extravagant Henry Owen Cunliffe. He proved to be its last occupant for he died impoverished in 1818, the estate was split up and the hall gradually fell into ruins. It is frequently alleged that Ferndean Manor in Charlotte Brontë's *Jane Eyre*

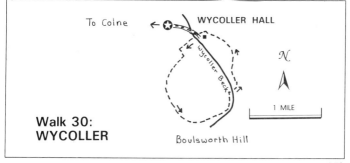

Walk 30: WYCOLLER

is based on Wycoller Hall, though there is no actual evidence. The proximity of Brontë Country is no doubt the main reason for this supposed connection.

The ruined hall, noted for its fine restored fireplaces, is a very atmospheric place, considerably enhanced by its setting in the middle of the village. The barn next door to it has been restored as a Country Park Information Centre and nearby is a picturesque pack-horse bridge and a simple clapper bridge, both dating back to the Middle Ages. What makes Wycoller so historically significant is that it has remained in a virtually fossilised state since the early 19th century, a rare example of an early industrial community that has neither grown into a large industrial town, nor become a desirable commuter area spoilt by modern residential development.

Route Directions
Follow the road from the car park down into the village and, opposite the ruined hall, turn right on to an uphill track signposted Raven Rock. You soon come to some farm buildings, go past them, climb a stile, turn left and at the end of the field go through the gate, turn right and head diagonally towards some railings around a walled pond. At this point there are excellent views over to Trawden, Colne and Pendle Hill to the right and the bare rugged moorlands of Boulsworth Hill to the left. Climb the stone steps in the wall in front, cross the farm track and continue through a gate and bear left towards the next farm. Go through a gap in the wall and carry on to the farm where you bear left and head in a straight line towards a house in front of Boulsworth Hill. Climb over a wall, head towards some stone steps in the next wall, pass in front of the farmhouse and then turn left along a track.

Follow the wide clear track along the base of Boulsworth Hill, go through a gate and bear left to join the main bridleway. Below you on the right is a miniature ravine and on the other side of it extensive views across the wild moorland that forms the edge of Brontë Country. After about one mile you drop down to cross the stream on your right, and continue on the other bank bearing right away from the stream. At the public footpath sign to Wycoller, climb the stile and head downhill towards a farm.

At the right-hand side of the farm climb a stile and turn right heading towards the next farm and a stile. Keeping to the left of the farm buildings, cross a footbridge and bear left uphill towards another farm. At this point the rocks of Foster's Leap are a prominent feature on the right. They get their name from Foster Cunliffe, a relation of a 17th century squire of Wycoller Hall who is alleged to have jumped across the gap between the two main rocks. Pass in front of the farm, turn right through a gate and continue by the side of a bungalow. From here it is an easy route back to Wycoller. Just follow the yellow waymarks across several fields and over several ladder-stiles. When you reach the distinctive upright stone slabs of the medieval vaccary walls turn left and follow the broad green track, the former coach drive to Wycoller Hall, down into the village.

Hardcastle Crags

31. HEPTONSTALL

Start and Finish: Heptonstall!
Distance: 5.5 miles   *Approximate Time:* 3 hours
Ordnance Survey Landranger Map: 103
Parking: Heptonstall
Refreshments: Pubs in Heptonstall

General Description
Spectacular moorland views, deep wooded ravines and a fascinating old handloom weavers' village set high above the Calder Valley are the varied ingredients of this walk. The way is easy to follow but, in this part of the south Pennines, inevitably involves some climbing. There are two main ascents: one fairly gentle but lengthy, the other short but steep.

Route Directions
From the village centre walk down Northgate following signs to the Methodist church and, just past the church, bear right along a rough
156

track. As you proceed downhill there are fine views over Hebden Bridge in the valley below. Continue down to a road, cross straight over and carry on in the same direction entering thick woodland. Where you join the main track, turn left and follow it through the woods, bearing round to the left and keeping parallel with Hebden Water below you on the right.

The valley becomes increasingly narrow and wooded and, just before a large house you make a sharp U-turn to the right and head down to the bridge at Midgehole. Cross over, turn left and then right where there is a public footpath sign to Haworth Old Road. For the next 1.25 miles it is a steady uphill climb as you follow the broad clear track above Crimsworth Dean, first through woodland and then into more open country with splendid moorland views. As you emerge into open country a farm is passed on the right and, about 0.25 mile further on, you turn left (just before a ruined farm building) and follow a wide grassy track enclosed by walls, still climbing. Go through a gate and, bearing slightly to the left, follow a clear, well-waymarked path across breezy heathery moorland with magnificent panoramic views. At first you keep by a wall on the left and, after passing through a gate, by the right-hand side of the wall. The path curves to the left gently downhill to enter the hamlet of Walshaw.

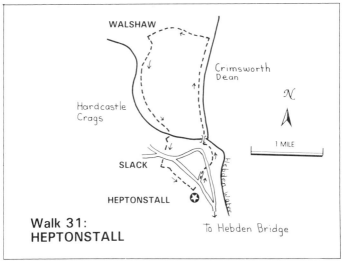

Walk 31:
HEPTONSTALL

Turn left along a tarmac road, over a stream and at a Y-junction take the right-hand fork and follow the track down into the wooded ravine of Hardcastle Crags. Hardcastle Crags is a popular National Trust beauty spot and contains some of the most attractive riverside walking in the Pennines. It is so reminiscent of Switzerland that for many years it was used as a meeting place for Swiss nationals living in England.

You pass on the right the rocks that give their name to the area and soon come to a deserted mill with some stepping stones nearby. Continue along the main track but soon turn right along a clear path that heads down to the stream and a second set of stepping stones. Cross the stream and take the zig-zag path opposite that climbs steeply, first to the right and then to the left, emerging from the woods at the top. Behind is a marvellous view over the steep-sided wooded ravine. Bear right and follow a straight walled path into the hamlet of Slack.

Cross straight over the road and take the path ahead by the side of a guest-house, through a gap in the wall on the right and between a wall on the left and fence on the right. Carry on across a field keeping by the fence on the right and at a T-junction of tracks, turn left along a wide grassy path. The tower of Heptonstall church can be seen in front and, for the rest of the way, there are magnificent views to the right over the Colden and Calder valleys. Bear left at a junction of tracks to join the Calderdale Way (well-waymarked with yellow arrows and CW signs) and follow these signs along a dramatic, rocky clifftop path high above the valley. At times the path is narrow and difficult to follow but keep to the high ground all the time, just below the ridge and by a wall on the left, and eventually you turn left along a walled track into Heptonstall.

Heptonstall

From the hilltop village you can look down on the jumble of mills and tall 'double-decker' houses of Hebden Bridge in the valley below. Hebden Bridge superseded Heptonstall as an industrial centre, leaving it high and dry (literally) as a fascinating example of a pre-Industrial Revolution textile community, with an appearance that can have changed little from the 18th century (apart from the Victorian church).

Heptonstall lay on one of the main trans-Pennine routeways from

Halifax to Burnley and many of its attractive rows of cottages date from the 17th and 18th centuries, the heyday of handloom weaving, when its population reached 4,000. It was the growth of water and steam-powered machinery during the Industrial Revolution that spelt doom for the handloom weavers and caused the woollen industry to move downhill to where the sources of energy lay at hand in the Calder Valley.

There is more to Heptonstall that just weavers' cottages, attractive as they are with their distinctive rows of upstairs windows made to give the weaver sufficient light. It has a Cloth Hall, first built in the Elizabethan period and remodelled in the 18th century. It is one of the few places in England that can boast two churches in one churchyard. The old ruined church, technically a chapel, dates mainly from the 15th century and its double nave makes it unusually wide. Over the centuries it took a battering from the winter gales that sweep across the Pennines and, after a severe storm in 1847 during which part of the tower was destroyed, it was decided to build a new church instead of repairing the old one. This new church, a fine example of Victorian Gothic, was opened in 1854. The ruins of the old church are very atmospheric and around them are hundreds of gravestones, including that of David 'King' Hartley, leader of a local gang who was hanged at York in 1770 for counterfeiting gold coins.

Another of Heptonstall's claims to fame is that it possesses the oldest Methodist chapel to have been in continuous use. It was built in 1764 and the foundation stone was laid by John Wesley himself, who incidentally disliked the old parish church and is alleged to have said in 1786: "I preached in Heptonstall Church, the Ugliest Church I know!" It has an octagonal shape which was common to Methodist chapels at the time, both to indicate that it was essentially a preaching house and to avoid giving offence to the Church of England.

On the south side of the churchyard the old grammar school founded in 1642 and rebuilt in 1771, now serves as a local museum.

Quarry Bank Mill at Styal

32. STYAL

Start and Finish: Styal (Quarry Bank Mill)
Distance: 4 miles   *Approximate Time:* 2 hours
Ordnance Survey Landranger Map: 109
Parking: Styal Country Park
Refreshments: Quarry Bank Mill

General Description
Combine a unique example of a purpose-built early Industrial Revolution textile community with attractive riverside woods and the result is a walk of great interest and variety that gives you a vivid insight into the way of life of a 19th century mill owner and his workforce. The walk is relatively short and easy to follow, but plenty of time needs to be devoted to exploring Styal village and Quarry Bank Mill at the end.

Route Directions
From the car park follow the signs down to Quarry Bank Mill and make

160

for a path on the right-hand side of the mill (signposted Morley). Cross the footbridge over the River Bollin and take the path straight ahead up through the woods. Go through a gate and keep straight on. Over to the right is a view of the steep-sided, thickly wooded Bollin Valley. Passing through another gate continue past the side of farm buildings and along the farm track to the Altrincham-Wilmslow road. Turn right and then first left into the hamlet of Morley. To the left the distinctive outline of Alderley Edge is clearly visible.

Morley contains some fine examples of half-timbered, black and white cottages. Go through the village and, where the road veers to the left, turn right along a broad track signposted to Castle Hill. At a stile bear left (following yellow waymarks) and at the next stile turn right along the edge of a field. On reaching a signpost turn sharp right, following signs to Oversley Ford, cross a stream, keep straight ahead across a field and, where the field ends, carry on to drop down steeply to the river bank. Turn right and follow the river up to the main road.

Go straight across the road and take the path by the side of a hotel car park to a bridge. Cross the bridge and turn right along the other bank of the river to re-enter Styal Country Park. For the next 2 miles you follow the river through the steep-sided and thickly wooded Bollin gorge. The woodland created by Robert Greg of nearby Quarry Bank Mill, a keen landscape gardener, in the middle of the 19th century, is most attractive but it is not an entirely relaxing stroll as there are quite a lot of steep climbs up and down. After a mile you cross a footbridge on to the opposite bank, and another 0.5 mile further on, cross another footbridge on the right, turn left and, ignoring the uphill

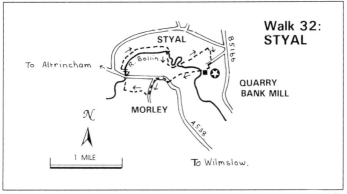

track that winds to the left, bear right to briefly rejoin the river bank. Soon you bear left away from the river to climb steeply through the woods. At the top of the ridge walk on and climb a stile near Norcliffe Chapel to enter Styal village.

The village is easy to explore as all the features of interest - the two chapels, Oak Cottages, shop, school and Farm Fold - are well-signposted from the village centre near the remains of the medieval cross. After visiting these follow the signposts for Quarry Bank Mill, no more than 0.5 mile away. The route takes you past the late 18th century Apprentice House, with its Victorian allotment, back to the car park and the mill building just beyond.

Quarry Bank Mill and Styal
In 1784 Samuel Greg, a Manchester cotton manufacturer, decided to build a large spinning mill on the banks of the River Bollin near Wilmslow where a fall in the river would provide power for the recently invented water-driven machines. From the start Quarry Bank Mill prospered and the original building was extended twice, a second water-wheel was added and the business was diversified when Samuel's son, Robert Greg, constructed weaving sheds in the 1830's. In its heyday the mill employed over 400 workers, but its very prosperity created problems. The neighbouring hamlet of Styal was too small to provide an adequate labour force and Samuel Greg was forced to recruit a large number of his workers from outside the area, often using pauper children from local workhouses. Accommodation and amenities had to be provided for them and this resulted in the transformation of Styal from a scattered, rural community into a purpose-built factory colony.

Next to the mill he built Quarry Bank House in 1796 as a home for his family, and the mill manager's house in 1810, both of which are private residences and not open to the public. Between the mill and village stands the Apprentice House, built in 1790 to house the 90-100 pauper apprentices that worked at Quarry Bank Mill, approximately one third of the entire workforce. Part of the garden of the Apprentice House has been made into a Victorian allotment where old varieties of vegetables are once more being grown.

Styal village retains some of its original thatched, black and white cottages, together with the remains of a medieval preaching cross, but most of it dates from the early 19th century when Samuel Greg had to provide housing for his large workforce. Initially he converted some of the barns into cottages and later built new rows of cottages, constructed to a much higher standard than most other workers houses at the time, with individual privies and gardens. Oak Farm Cottages are fine examples of these. An unusually wide range of amenities was also provided. In 1823 a school was built both for the local village and factory children, pre-dating by ten years the legislation that made some form of factory schooling compulsory. A village shop was established, later taken over by the local co-operative society but closed down in the 1960's. As there was no church at Styal religious needs also had to be catered for. At first the apprentices had to walk across the fields twice on Sunday to the parish church at Wilmslow, but in 1822 Samuel Greg, himself a Nonconformist, built the Unitarian Oak Chapel, (later renamed Norcliffe Chapel), and in 1837 a waggon house at Farm Fold was converted into a Methodist chapel.

Quarry Bank Mill ceased production in 1959 and today it is run by a charitable trust on lease from the National Trust. It is a most striking building and shows that industrial structures do not have to be ugly or badly designed. Perhaps its most attractive feature is the classical bell tower, essential to ensure good timekeeping among the workforce. Inside it is a fascinating working museum showing the development of the factory system in the cotton industry. You are shown the counting house and mill manager's office, there are displays illustrating the life of the mill owners and their workers and demonstrations of old textile machinery.

Despite the inevitably harsh conditions at the mill: long hours, low wages, strict discipline, child labour, etc., Samuel Greg was considerably more enlightened than most of his contemporaries. He was way ahead of his time in catering for the domestic, educational and spiritual needs of his workers and even employed a medical officer to look after the health of his apprentices. In 1939 one of his descendants gave Quarry Bank Mill, the village and surrounding woods to the National Trust and they now form the Styal Country Park. Together they make up an unusually complete and rare surviving example of a self-contained mill community of the early Industrial Revolution; almost entirely the creation of one man and unspoilt by later development - a living museum of social history.

Higher Mill at Helmshore

33. HELMSHORE TEXTILE MUSEUMS

Start and Finish: Helmshore
Distance: 5 miles   *Approximate Time:* 2hrs 30 mins
Ordnance Survey Landranger Map: 103
Parking: Helmshore Textile Museums
Refreshments: Pubs in Helmshore, café at the museum

General Description
Away from the industrialised and urbanised valley bottoms, early centres of both the woollen and cotton industries, the Forest of Rossendale is still an area of open, hilly and lonely moorland with extensive views. This walk combines two very different facets of Rossendale's varied history: a walk through part of a medieval deer park and a visit to two adjoining mills, now housing early machinery and displays illustrating the development of the Lancashire textile industry.

Forest of Rossendale
Despite its name Rossendale, like some other neighbouring Lancashire

forests (Trawden, Pendle, Bowland), was not a forest but a chase. The difference in the two titles is that a forest was an area in which the king had sole hunting rights whereas in a chase those rights belonged to a private individual, usually a baron or bishop. Rossendale was part of the 'Honour of Clitheroe', a vast area of land stretching from the Ribble to the Mersey, and for much of the Middle Ages belonged to the powerful de Lacy family of Clitheroe Castle.

It originally covered much of the area between Accrington, Darwen and Bacup, a wild and unbroken area of open moorland intersected by wooded valleys and with few settlements. At the end of the Middle Ages it was disafforested and it was about this time that the first small woollen industries appeared although even as late as the 19th century, it remained a largely remote and sparsely populated area.

Route Directions

From the museum car park turn right along the road, and just past a row of cottages called Park Lane View, turn sharp left up a hilly track (public footpath sign to Musbury Heights) which climbs behind the cottages. Bear right to a gate, climb a stile and continue past a ruined farmhouse to another stile, climb over and turn right along a track to a farm.

Keep to the left of the farm and continue along a narrow path that squeezes between a wall on the left and hedge on the right. Climb a

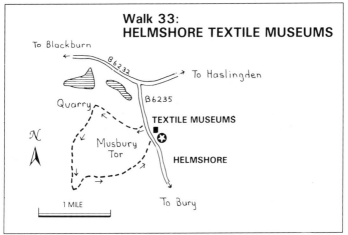

Walk 33:
HELMSHORE TEXTILE MUSEUMS

stile, carry straight on and, where the wall ends, continue to join a broad track where there is a public footpath sign. Where the track bends right to a farm cross over the stile in front and walk along the uphill track with a stone wall on the right. Over to the right are fine views over the Grane Valley with the reservoirs immediately below. Continue climbing all the time, to go through a disused quarry and eventually reach a gate.Quarrying was another important Rossendale industry, the stone was prized as paving slabs.

Go through the gate and turn left to follow a clear path between the spoil heaps of the quarry to the boundary wall. You are now on the Rossendale Way, a circular waymarked trail around the Rossendale Valley. Climb a stile and in front there is a superb view of the wild, open, and perhaps surprisingly, unspoilt Musbury Valley with the prominent landmark of Musbury Tor slightly to the left. Continue along the clear path ahead that follows the side of the valley, past several ruined farms, giving fine views all the time. This area of the forest was enclosed by Henry de Lacy in 1305 to form a deer park and the boundary of Musbury Park, a ditch running parallel to the path on the right, can be easily seen. Later the ditch turns abruptly left and you can see it heading across the moorland towards the slopes of the Tor.

After a mile the path veers round the head of the valley, over a stream, down through a mini gorge, over another stream and turns left to head back along the other side of the valley, bearing right uphill. Eventually it levels out and, at a stile by a gate, you climb over and keep on along a clear path across a large field. At this stage there are fine views all around. Go through a gate and continue across the next field, passing a small plantation on the right, and later joining a stone wall on the right. Go through another gate, walk down a concrete drive towards a farm but at the next gate bear half-left along the side of a wall on the right.

The path keeps by the wall and goes across the shoulder of Musbury Tor. Climb a stile, carry on, go over a ladder-stile and turn sharp right by a wall. Climb another stile and turn left along a track by farm buildings. Go through a gate and ahead is a superb view over Helmshore, Haslingden and the Rossendale Valley. Squeeze through the gap in the wall ahead and walk downhill across the field in the direction of the prominent mill chimney. On reaching a winding, walled track turn right and follow it down to the road where you turn left to the buildings of the textile museums.

Helmshore Textile Museums

The woollen industry was established first in Rossendale in the 16th century, cotton came later in the 18th century. Rossendale possessed a number of advantages as a textile manufacturing area: sheep rearing on the local hills, a damp climate and proximity to the major cotton centres of Liverpool and Manchester. Its advantages became even more obvious during the Industrial Revolution: plenty of fast-flowing streams when water-powered machinery was introduced, and local coal supplies when steam-powered machines were invented. As a result it became a major textile region in the 19th century when mills were built all along the valleys and the neighbouring towns expanded rapidly. The decline of both cotton and wool since the First World War has led to closure, and either the demolition or adaptation of many mill buildings. Two adjoining mills here at Helmshore have been converted into a unique museum of the Lancashire textile industry.

Of the two buildings, one (Higher Mill) was a late 18th century woollen fulling mill and the other, larger one (Whitaker's Mill) was built in the early 19th century as a cotton spinning mill. The exact relationship between them is unclear: they appear to have been two quite separate undertakings but, most of the time, under the same ownership. They were not physically linked until after the creation of the museum.

The Turner family were largely responsible for the development of Helmshore in the early 19th century. They built Higher Mill in 1789, one of the earliest fulling mills in Rossendale. Fulling is a process whereby the woollen cloth is subjected to pressure and moisture to form heavy material suitable for blankets etc. At one time stale urine was used to break down the grease in the cloth prior to fulling, but later chemicals were used, avoiding the necessity to go round and collect quantities of urine from local houses. After the fulling process the cloth had to be 'tentered' , i.e. straightened and dried. At first this was done outside where the cloth was placed on tenterhooks (the origin of the phrase) but later the drying was done inside by a steam process.

William Turner (1793-1852) was an enterprising businessman. As well as improving Higher Mill he built the adjoining three storey building in the early 19th century as a steam-powered cotton spinning mill, though it had to be rebuilt in 1859-60 after a disastrous fire. Both mills passed to the Whitaker family who ran them until the late 1960's.

The two museums have a large collection of early textile machinery and displays showing the development of the textile industries. There is a lot to see here and a visit provides a fascinating insight into Rossendale's past and the rise and fall of the industry which will always be associated with Lancashire.

Sir Titus Salt's monumental mill at Saltaire

34. ILKLEY AND SALTAIRE

Start: Ilkley   *Finish:* Shipley
Distance: 7.5 miles   *Approximate Time:* 4 hours
Ordnance Survey Landranger Map: 104
Parking: Ilkley
Refreshments: Pubs, restaurant and cafés in Ilkley, Dick Hudson's Inn (about half-way point), pub and café at Shipley Glen, Boat House Restaurant at Saltaire

General Description
Starting from Ilkley you climb out of the Wharfe Valley, across the breezy and heathery expanses of world-famous Ilkley Moor, to drop down into the Aire Valley at Saltaire via the thickly-wooded beauty spot of Shipley Glen. Saltaire provides the major historic interest - a rare and fascinating example of a planned, model Victorian textile community created by one man, Sir Titus Salt, whose benign influence still dominates the entire place.

Ilkley
Ilkley is a town with a long history. It was originally the Roman fort of

Olicana, one of a chain between Ribchester and York, later a medieval farming settlement, in the 18th and 19th centuries a spa and, after the coming of the railway, a favourite residential area for the 'wool barons' of nearby Leeds and Bradford.

Evidence of these different facets of the town's development can be seen both at the start and during the first part of the walk. The site of the Roman fort is a flat rectangular area in the town centre above the River Wharfe, now occupied by the medieval parish church and predominantly 17th century manor house, both of which are well worth a visit. The church contains some Anglo-Saxon crosses and the manor house now serves as an interesting local museum. A walk around the town reveals a number of examples of Victorian and Edwardian architecture - public buildings, shopping streets and arcades, churches and the imposing hotels that were built in Ilkley's heyday as a health resort. The first baths that created the spa are passed soon after the start of the walk.

Route Directions (Ilkley to Saltaire)

It is now time to make your way onto 'Ilkla Moor'. From the crossroads near the station walk up Wells Road towards the moor which looms ahead. The famous song, Yorkshire's national anthem and favourite 'party piece' of many after a night at the pub, was allegedly composed by a church choir during an outing and picnic on the moor.

Just before a cattle-grid bear left for a few yards, through a gate, up some steps by a pond and along a path ascending towards a white building in front. This is White Wells, built in 1756 to house two open air baths (the roof was added later), thus beginning Ilkley's development as a spa. Nowadays it is a museum on health cures and spa treatments. Continue up the steps behind and bear left along a broad path towards the prominent landmark of Ilkley Crags. All the way there are superb views across the moor, and to the left and behind over the town and the Wharfe Valley. Bear right up steps at the side of the crags and continue for the next mile along a clear path marked by cairns, climbing steadily all the time to the highest point near a prehistoric stone circle on the left. Ilkley Moor is littered with stone circles and rock carvings of various ages, Bronze Age, Celtic, Saxon and Viking.

Now the path flattens out and starts to descend gently towards a stile in the wall ahead. Climb over and continue until you reach a gate

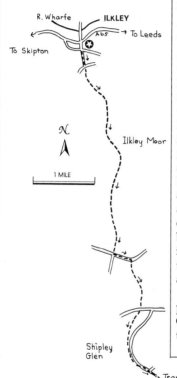

**Walk 34:
ILKLEY and
SALTAIRE**

R. Wharfe   **ILKLEY**
                        → To Leeds
To Skipton   A65

𝒩
⋀

1 MILE

Ilkley Moor

Shipley
Glen

Tramway
R. Aire
SALTAIRE
To Keighley ←   **SHIPLEY**
                      → To Leeds
Leeds and Liverpool Canal

in another wall. Go through and in front you get a fine view over the Aire Valley. Keep on and you soon leave the moor behind as you climb a stile and walk down a rocky walled path to reach the road opposite Dick Hudson's Inn. Turn left along the road for just under 0.5 mile and, by the side of The Croft Restaurant, turn right along a farm track. Where the track swings sharply to the left keep straight on through a gate and across a field (wall on right) to a gate and stile. Bear slightly left across the next field (following blue waymarks) to another gate and stile from where you get a view of the open expanses of Baildon Moor in front. Climb over and walk on, cross another stile and follow the path to the right over a stile to a farm. Keeping the buildings on your right, turn left in front of the farmhouse along the drive, through a gate and over a stile to the road.

Cross over and take the footpath opposite (signposted to The Glen). Climb a stile and follow the path which squeezes between a fence on the left and stream on the right, over another stile and carries on. After a while you drop down into a small wooded dell where you climb a stile and then, bearing slightly to the left away from the stream, walk across an area of rough grass and fern drawing parallel to the road on your left. Now you follow the wide verge by the side of the road for nearly 0.75 mile along the edge of the steep, rocky, thickly-wooded Shipley Glen, a popular local walking and picnic area, as far as the Old Glen House pub and adjacent café.

Here you take to the road for a short distance and, where it ends at the amusement area at the top of the Shipley Glen Tramway, keep on and either follow the side of the tramway down through the woods, or if it is running, give your legs a rest by taking the short ride on the cable-hauled tramway. It was first opened in 1895 and, after a number of financial and vandalism problems over the years, was restored and re-opened in 1982. From the bottom station continue along the path to the road where you turn left and shortly right, through a gap in the wall, to enter Roberts Park. Turn right along the path running parallel to the road, turning left soon and making for the statue of Sir Titus Salt, creator of Saltaire. From the terrace by the statue there is a superb view of the enormous mill and imposing church, the two most outstanding of Sir Titus's buildings. Continue down the steps at the side of the statue and turn left to follow a path up to the bridge over the River Aire.

Saltaire

In many ways Sir Titus Salt was a typical Victorian businessman; self-made and successful woollen magnate, strict Nonconformist, devoted husband and father (of eleven children) and local politician (Mayor of Bradford). In one way, however, he was not typical because he was also a philanthropist who, when he decided to build a new large mill to replace his four existing ones, also planned a new community for his workers.

He chose a site with the advantages of being situated on the River Aire, the Leeds-Liverpool canal and the railway. Construction began in 1853 and the result was Saltaire: a model purpose-built, mill village far in advance of its time as regards both standard of housing and provision of amenities for its inhabitants.

The park, final touch of the new community (opened in 1871) has already been seen. Before leaving the park note the Boat House Restaurant just by the bridge, with its riverside terrace and authentic

Victorian dining room. The rest of Saltaire's attractions can be seen by taking a short stroll along Victoria Road as far as the main Bradford-Keighley road. On the left-hand side you pass, in this order, the mill, Saltaire Club and Institute (now Victoria Hall) opened in 1871 as a social centre, the hospital and alms houses. Returning down the other side you pass more alms houses with gardens, the factory school and the church. As you can see Sir Titus catered for all the needs of his employees bar one - as a strict Congregationalist he would not allow alcohol to be sold anywhere in his new village.

All the buildings were constructed from the same light-coloured stone and the major ones were built on a monumental scale, especially the mill and church. The mill is a colossal building covering an area of 55,000 feet, once employing 2,500 workers and with an ornamental chimney 250 feet high. Built in a Venetian Gothic style it resembles a grand Italian palace. The Congregational (now United Reformed) church, completed in 1858, is also built in an Italian style, but classical instead of Gothic. It appropriately contains the tombs of Sir Titus Salt and his family.

A walk around Saltaire is a fascinating experience, an insight into the more benevolent and paternalistic side of 19th century capitalism, and a rare example of a self-contained, purpose-built industrial village.

Route Directions (Saltaire to Shipley)
The final stretch of the walk, about 1 mile, is along the canal bank, under Victoria Road bridge and through the middle of the mill complex. There is an interestingly varied mixture of old and modern industrial buildings by the canal, with some of the older mills and warehouses now converted to other uses.

Turn right over the second bridge and up the road to the traffic lights in the centre of Shipley. Here you can catch a bus or a train back to Ilkley. Details from Ilkley Tourist Information Office (0943 602319).

Ribblehead Viaduct backed by Whernside

35. RIBBLEHEAD VIADUCT

Start and Finish: Ribblehead
Distance: 7 miles   *Approximate Time:* 3hrs 30 mins
Ordnance Survey Landranger Map: 98
Parking: Opposite Station Inn at Ribblehead
Refreshments: Station Inn at Ribblehead, Old Hill Inn near Chapel-le-Dale

General Description
The Settle-Carlisle line is justly renowned as one of the most spectacular railway journeys in Britain, and one of the major engineering triumphs of the Victorian era. This walk, amidst the wild and dramatic landscape of the Three Peaks of Pen-y-ghent, Ingleborough and Whernside, is dominated for most of the way by the Ribblehead Viaduct, the most impressive structure on the line, which carries the railway across the bleak expanses at the head of Ribblesdale. Such a feat of engineering was not achieved without considerable human cost - a fact which becomes apparent during the course of the walk.

Settle-Carlisle Railway and Ribblehead Viaduct
During the railway mania of the 19th century the directors of the Midland Railway Company were anxious to share in the profitable

traffic between London and Scotland, then monopolised by the London and North-Western Railway and North-Eastern Railway. After various failed negotiations with other companies they decided to construct a new route between Leeds and Carlisle via Skipton, Settle and Appleby. The route was to follow the valleys of the Ribble and Eden, with a middle section between the heads of the two valleys crossing some of the wildest Pennine moorland.

The construction of the Settle-Carlisle section of the line, between 1869 and 1875, was a prodigious feat of engineering. The problems were immense - difficult terrain involving the building of long tunnels and viaducts, inhospitable surroundings and sometimes atrocious weather. Added to this were the enormous organisational difficulties of mobilising and keeping together the labour force needed to carry out the task.

A large army of navvies - many of them Scots and Irish - were employed and hastily constructed accommodation had to be provided for them at intervals along the line. Shanty towns sprang up which seem to have resembled the gold mining and cattle towns of the American West, both in appearance and atmosphere. Women and children accompanied the navvies and fighting, drunkenness, poaching and rioting seem to have been fairly commonplace. At the same time the largest of these temporary settlements, Batty Green (which housed nearly 2,000 people), possessed a school, mission house, hospital, library and post office. Inevitably such living and working conditions led to many accidents and a huge loss of life.

The most impressive single feature of the line is the mighty Ribblehead Viaduct, nearly 0.25 mile long and reaching to a maximum height of 106 feet. It is a tribute, not only to the engineering skills of the Victorians but also to their aesthetic qualities, that this structure blends in with its wild and bleak surroundings and seems to be almost part of the landscape (some might say it even enhances it). It resembles some of the great Roman aqueducts that can still be seen in Spain and southern France.

The Settle-Carlisle line remains the outstanding constructional achievement of the Victorian 'Railway Age' and a ride along it, especially in good weather, is a memorable experience.

Route Directions (Ribblehead to Chapel-le-Dale)
Opposite the car park and by the side of the inn is a broad, clear track

that heads across rough grassland towards the viaduct. As you walk along it you get a marvellous view of the viaduct, backed by the slopes of Whernside. The open and treeless scenery around here is bleak but, at the same time, both impressive and appealing and makes an interesting contrast with the gentler and more wooded landscape as you proceed down the dale.

Follow the track as its winds under the massive arches of the viaduct, keep on through a gate and past farm buildings to a footbridge over Waterscales Beck. Cross over and turn left through a gate to follow a tarmac farm road through several gates, eventually bearing left to join another farm road coming in from the right. Re-cross the beck and continue, with a superb view of Ingleborough in front, as far as a gate by the side of a cattle-grid. Here you bear right away from the road (public bridleway sign to Philpin Lane), cross grass and by a wall on your right up to a gate. Go through and carry on by a wall on the left. At the corner of the wall continue to cross the usually dry bed of the stream, making for a ladder-stile in front.

Climb over and walk on, veering slightly to the left, to a gate. Go through and walk along the narrow rocky path, between a wall on the right and fence on the left, to a tarmac farm road. Turn left and follow it up to the B6255 (Ingleton-Hawes road). Over the last mile you will have noticed a gradual change of scenery from the bleakness and openness around Ribblehead to a more gentle, wooded landscape of bright green fields divided by drystone walls.

Turn right at the road (Old Hill Inn is a few yards to the left) and

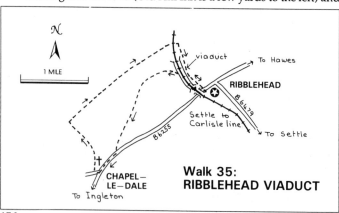

Walk 35: RIBBLEHEAD VIADUCT

follow it downhill into the hamlet of Chapel-le-Dale, turning right along a lane and over a stream to the church.

Chapel-le-Dale
This tiny church in its attractive tranquil setting, originally a chapel and given parish church status in 1864, reminds us of the darker side of the building of the Settle-Carlisle Railway. During its construction the bodies of navvies killed on the job, plus women and children who died in the conditions of the shanty towns, were brought here for burial. It is estimated that over 200 people lie in unmarked graves in the churchyard and inside is a memorial to all those who lost their lives in the building of the railway.

Route Directions (Chapel-le-Dale to Ribblehead)
Turn right up the narrow lane that passes the front of the church, keep on through a gate (passing Hurtle Pot on the right) and, where the road ends, continue along a broad track (signposted to Ellerbeck) up through a most attractive, rocky, tree-lined pass. Passing a bronze statue of a man (retrieved from Hurtle Pot) continue upwards into open country with extensive views all around, including distant glimpses of Ribblehead Viaduct on the right and a particularly striking view of Whernside. Bear right to cross a beck at a public footpath sign to Deepdale and follow the track which winds past farm buildings, veering right to a gate.

After going through the gate you proceed along a clear wide track, past several farms and through several gates, which follows the lower slopes of Whernside and gives superb views over the dale towards the viaduct. After about 1.5 miles the track swings sharply to the left. At this point keep straight on for a few yards to a stile (public bridleway sign to Winterscales), climb over and continue across the grass towards farm buildings. Go through a gate and carry on in front of the buildings and across the field, parallel to a wall on the left, to a gate. Go through and walk on to the next gate, through that and straight across the middle of the field to another gate. Now you get a good view over on the right of the third of the Three Peaks, Pen-y-ghent. Go through and ahead, over a footbridge towards a house in front and, keeping by a fence and wall on the right, go through a gate and cross to the farm buildings in front.

Continue through two gates and the middle of the farm buildings to a tarmac track which you follow to the next group of farm buildings. Cross the bridge over the stream and keep on along a stony track to a gate. Go through and bear left, following the stream, towards Blea Moor signal box in front. Bear right under the railway bridge and turn right to pick up a track running parallel to the railway.

The final stretch of the walk gives excellent views of all the Three Peaks plus the viaduct - a mixture of natural and man-made wonders to provide a fitting climax. Climb a stile by a gate and shortly afterwards bear left away from the main track along a narrow path which soons bears right across rough grass. Keep by the side of the viaduct to pick up the broad, well-surfaced track which leads back to the Station Inn and car park.

Restored canal side warehouses at Wigan Pier - the original pier is in the foreground on the right

36. WIGAN PIER

Start and Finish: Wigan Pier
Distance: 4 miles   *Approximate Time:* 2 hours
Ordnance Survey Landranger Map: 108
Parking: Wigan Pier - clearly signposted from all main roads into Wigan
Refreshments: Pub and café at Wigan Pier

General Description

To suggest a walk in the Wigan area a few years ago would have been considered as big a joke as Wigan Pier itself. However, the decline of many of the traditional 19th century industries has enabled nature to re-assert itself and, on a number of formerly grimy and derelict industrial sites, green countryside is starting to appear once more. Such changes can be observed on this short walk along the banks of the Leeds-Liverpool Canal from Wigan Pier to Wigan Flashes, a series of shallow lakes formed from mining subsidence which, together with their ex-colliery surroundings, create a pleasant rural environment. This is a walk through a post-industrial landscape, a clear reminder that our landscape is both a chiefly man-made and an ever-changing phenomenon.

Route Directions

It is probably preferable to do the walk first and get an idea of the local landscape in order to enjoy and appreciate better the imaginative new Wigan Pier Museum at the end.

Therefore make your way across the road from the car park to the canal, turn left past The Orwell Restaurant, right over the bridge and right again along the opposite bank. As you continue down a ramp the actual site of the original Wigan Pier, a coal staithe on the canal, can be seen about 100 yards ahead, marked by a raised section of the path and a short piece of waggon way. Turn left under the bridge and walk along the canal towpath past the vast and imposing Trencherfield Mill, another part of the Wigan Pier complex and also probably best visited at the end of the walk, along with all the other attractions.

Continue along the canal past Trencherfield Gardens up to a road bridge. Turn right over the bridge and left along the other bank of the canal. Over to the left is a row of attractive, restored canalside cottages. You soon come to a canal junction where you keep right along the towpath, following the Leigh branch of the Leeds-Liverpool Canal built in 1820 to provide access to Manchester via the Bridgewater Canal. Keep ahead, parallel with a road on the right and past cooling

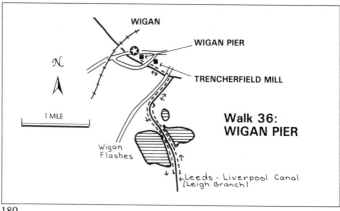

towers on the left, to quickly emerge into semi-rural surroundings.

After just over 0.5 mile you reach the start of a series of expanses of shallow water called the Wigan Flashes, created from depressions caused by mining subsidence. Much of the surrounding area once comprised coal mines but the tips have been landscaped and re-planted, and the flashes and surrounding marshland have become a popular area for wildlife, thus creating a pleasant environment out of what was a derelict industrial wasteland. Across the waters on the horizon you can see the line of low hills stretching towards St. Helens and Ormskirk.

When you have reached the far end of the large flash on your right, turn left over a footbridge, left again and walk back along the opposite bank. The canal cuts across the middle of two flashes and in front you can see the buildings of Wigan. Look out for a church on the left and, at this point, turn left to re-cross the canal. Turn right and retrace your steps to Wigan Pier.

Wigan Pier

It was the presence of local coal deposits and the proximity of the cotton industry that led to the industrial development of Wigan. This development was furthered by the construction of the Leeds-Liverpool Canal (1770-1816) which runs through the middle of the town. The canal, together with its later extension to Leigh and the Bridgewater Canal, made Wigan the centre of a communications network radiating to Manchester, the Mersey, the Ribble, the cotton towns of north-east Lancashire and across the Pennines to Leeds and the woollen towns of Yorkshire. The actual pier, a music hall joke first invented by the elder George Formby and popularised by George Orwell in his book of that name, was simply a staithe on the canal bank from which coal waggons were tipped into the waiting barges; its site can be seen just opposite the main exhibition building.

In time cotton declined, the coal mines closed down, the canal traffic dwindled and the mills, wharfs and warehouses were abandoned and became derelict. Now this stretch of canal has been given a new lease of life because of the recent development of the Wigan Pier Museum and exhibition complex comprising 'The Way We Were' Heritage Centre, a pub and restaurant, shop and offices and the Trencherfield Mill, plus canalside gardens, walks and boat trips.

The highlight of any visit is a tour of 'The Way We Were' Heritage

The highlight of any visit is a tour of 'The Way We Were' Heritage Centre which, by a series of authentic and vivid displays and exhibits, seeks to convey how the ordinary people of Wigan and its locality lived, worked, played and died in the year 1900. Here you can experience life in the mines and mills, shops and pubs of the time. Here you can appreciate the strict discipline in the schools, the heartbreak of bereavement and the pleasures of a rail trip to the seaside. Particularly imaginative is the Victorian schoolroom, if you participate here make sure that your fingernails are clean!

A short distance away is Trencherfield Mill, already passed twice on the walk. You can get there by waterbus which, as well as saving your legs, is a pleasant way of travelling and part of the whole Wigan Pier experience. Here the chief attraction is to watch the mighty steam engine in operation - a truly awe-inspiring sight.

By following this walk, and visiting the varied offerings of Wigan Pier at the end of it, you get an idea of some of the possible solutions to the problems of derelict industrial landscapes and redundant industrial buildings.

CICERONE PRESS BOOKS

Cicerone publish a range of guides to walking and climbing in Britain and other general interest books

LAKE DISTRICT
LAKELAND VILLAGES
WORDSWORTH'S DUDDON REVISITED
REFLECTIONS ON THE LAKES
THE WESTMORLAND HERITAGE WALK
THE HIGH FELLS OF LAKELAND
IN SEARCH OF WESTMORLAND
CONISTON COPPER MINES - A Field Guide
CONISTER COPPER - A History
SCRAMBLES IN THE LAKE DISTRICT
WINTER CLIMBS IN THE LAKE DISTRICT
THE REGATTA MEN
LAKELAND - A Taste to Remember. (Recipes)
THE CHRONICLES OF MILNTHORPE
WALKS IN SILVERDALE/ARNSIDE - Area of Outstanding Natural Beauty
BIRDS OF MORECAMBE BAY
THE EDEN WAY - OUR CUMBRIA
PETTIE (Memories of a Victorian Nursery)

NORTHERN ENGLAND
THE YORKSHIRE DALES
LAUGHS ALONG THE PENNINE WAY (Cartoons)
THE RIBBLE WAY
NORTH YORK MOORS
WALKING THE CLEVELAND WAY AND MISSING LINK
WALKS ON THE WEST PENNINE MOORS
WALKING NORTHERN RAILWAYS - Vol.1. East Vol.2. West
BIRDS OF MERSEYSIDE
ROCK CLIMBS IN LANCASHIRE AND THE NORTH WEST
THE ISLE OF MAN COASTAL PATH
HERITAGE TRAILS IN NORTH WEST ENGLAND

DERBYSHIRE PEAK DISTRICT
WHITE PEAK WALKS Vol. 1 & 2
HIGH PEAK WALKS
WHITE PEAK WAY
KINDER LOG

WALES
THE RIDGES OF SNOWDONIA
HILL WALKING IN SNOWDONIA
ASCENT OF SNOWDON
WELSH WINTER CLIMBS
MOUNTAIN SUMMITS OF WALES
SNOWDONIA , WHITE WATER, SEA & SURF

WELSH BORDER
ROCK CLIMBS IN THE WEST MIDLANDS

SOUTH & WEST ENGLAND
WALKS IN KENT
THE WEALDWAY & VANGUARD WAY
THE SOUTH DOWNS WAY & DOWNS LINK
WALKING ON DARTMOOR
SOUTH WEST WAY - Vol. 1 & 2

SCOTLAND
SCRAMBLES IN LOCHABER
SCRAMBLES IN SKYE
ROCK CLIMBS: GLEN NEVIS & LOCHABER OUTCROPS
THE ISLAND OF RHUM
CAIRNGORMS, WINTER CLIMBS
WINTER CLIMBS BEN NEVIS & GLENCOE
SCOTTISH RAILWAY WALKS

Also a full range of guide-books to walking, scrambling, ice-climbing, rock climbing, and other adventurous pursuits in Britain and abroad.

Available from bookshops, outdoor equipment shops or direct (send for price list) from: CICERONE PRESS, 2 POLICE SQUARE, MILNTHORPE, CUMBRIA LA7 7PY

Printed by Carnmor Print & Design,
95/97, London Road, Preston, Lancashire.